THE EVOLUTION OF BRITISH POLICY TOWARDS INDIAN STATES, 1774-1858.

THE EVOLUTION OF BRITISH POLICY TOWARDS INDIAN STATES, 1774-1858.

(THE CALCUTTA UNIVERSITY READERSHIP LECTURES, 1929.)

BY

K. M. PANIKKAR, B.A.

GYAN

Published by

GYAN

Gyan Publishing House
5, Ansari Road
Daryaganj, New Delhi-110002
Phone: 011-47034999, 9811692060
E-mail: books@gyanbooks.com

Distribution Network
gyanbooks.com
India, USA, Canada, UK, Australia

ISBN: 978-81-212-8450-9 (HB)
First Published, 1929

2nd Impression 2024

Printed at: Gyan Press, Delhi.

THE EVOLUTION OF BRITISH POLICY TOWARDS INDIAN STATES, 1774-1858
Author: K. M. PANIKKAR

THE EVOLUTION OF BRITISH POLICY TOWARDS INDIAN STATES, 1774-1858.

(The Calcutta University Readership Lectures, 1929)

BY

K. M. PANIKKAR, B.A. (Oxon.), Bar-at-Law

READER TO THE CALCUTTA UNIVERSITY

Member of the American Academy of Political and Social Science,
Deputy Director of Special Organisation of the Chamber of Princes.
Author of "The Relation Between Government of India and the Indian States" "Sri Harsha of Kanauj", "Malabar and the Portuguese," Etc.

PUBLISHED UNDER THE AUTHORITY O
THE CALCUTTA UNIVERSITY

BY

S. K. LAHIRI & CO.

CALCUTTA

CONTENTS

INTRODUCTION

The subject I have chosen for these lectures is entitled the *Evolution of British Policy towards Indian States from 1774 to 1858*. I should like to make it clear at the very start that these lectures are not meant to cover the history of the period indicated. My purpose is only to trace the gradual evolution of a definite policy towards Indian States. It is therefore only with an aspect of British Indian history that I am concerned. It is true that the aspect I have chosen is not only an important aspect but one that provides the clue for the interpretation of the general policy of the Company. This may seem to be an extravagant claim, but when it is remembered that the relations with Indian States constituted the foreign policy of the Company, and the establishment of the British Empire in India outside Bengal was the gradual outcome of that policy, the claim will no doubt be granted by all fair-minded critics.

Though the importance of this aspect of Indian history is therefore undeniable, so far it has been neglected both by our historians and by our Universities. Of isolated events and incidents, or in relation to individual States, we have many admirable monographs. Thus with regard to the relation of the Company with Hyderabad, we have Brigg's excellent book, '*The Nizam, his history and relation with the British Government,*' and Frazer's '*Nizam, our Faithful Ally.*' With regard to the Gaekwar again there is an interesting monograph by Colonel Wallace entitled the '*Gaekwar and his realtions with the British Government.*' Hope's '*House of Scindia,*' Cunningham's '*History of the Sikhs,*' Basu's '*Story of Satara*' and numerous other books deal with the relations of the British Government with individual States. The State papers of Gwalior have been arranged by Parasnis and published under the authority of Scindia's Government. The pecuniary transactions of Messrs. Palmer & Co., can be read with interest in the blue book published by the East India Company, and there are numerous parliamentary papers dealing with Oudh, Carnatic, Baroda, Hyderabad and Mysore. The general problem of subsidiary alliance is dealt with by B. S. Jones in a book entitled *'Papers relating to the progress of British power in India and the system of subsidiary alliance.'* From the point of view of different Governors-General also there is much material available dealing with their administration. Warren Hastings wrote a long and detailed justification of his policy towards the States. The policy of Wellesley was defended in enthusiastic memoranda by his distinguished brother the Duke of Wellington and in our own days by Sydney Owen. But the best interpretation of his policy is contained in his own despatches and in the Wellesley manuscripts preserved in the British Museum. Those who are anxious to understand the policy of the Marquis of Hastings may turn with profit to his private journals and to his biography. His work in India is also the subject of an elaborate disquisition by Princep entitled *'The Military and Political Transactions in India during the Administration of the Marquis of Hastings.'* The administration of Dalhousie which came in for much criticism has had its apologists in the Duke of Argylle and in Sir William Lee-Warner, while a different point of view will be found in Sir Edwin Arnold's book *'The Administration of Dalhousie.'* The principal actors on the stage of Indian State policy have also left voluminous material. Malcolm has a biography to himself—besides his report on Malwa and his instructions to Political Officers. The lives of Metcalfe and Mount Stuart Elphinstone and the select writings of that statesman and soldier, and of Sir Thomas Munro, are also books well known to the student of Indian History.

Thus there is no dearth of published material for a connected study of British policy towards the States for the period which we have selected. But so far no one has attempted it. Nor do I claim that these lectures provide such a study. In so short a course as 6 lectures it is impossible to attempt anything more than an outline; but I hope that outline would be sufficiently clear and would bring out the essentials of a policy which by the circumstances of Indian historical growth was at all times complicated by numerous side-issues and the widely differing temperaments and character of the Governors-General and of the administrative officers entrusted with the conduct of that policy, but which none the less had a significant unity from the very beginning.

An official definition of an Indian State occurs in a Convention with the French Government (quoted in the 3rd schedule of the Indian Act No. VII of 1871), where it is defined as any State in India which is under the protection or political control of Her Majesty or of which the Government has acknowledged the supremacy of the British Crown.

No such State existed in India in 1774. In 1858 all the States in India except Nepal had come to occupy the position as defined above. What we shall attempt in the following lectures is first, to see how this transformation was brought about, and secondly, what policy was followed towards these States during the period we have chosen. The complicated nature of the problem precludes any simple formula of 'open sesame' to be applied to this system. The transformation of Indian States was partly by force of circumstances and partly by the pressure of irresistible currents of history; and the policy towards them was evolved partly by the official character of the East India Company, partly by the views and ambitions of Governors-General, but mainly by the conviction which developed with Wellesley and continued up to our own time that the Government of the whole of India directly or indirectly by the British is part of a pre-ordained system. These we shall discuss in the main body of my lectures. It is sufficient for me here to indicate the scope of these discourses and the limits which I have placed on myself.

It remains for me now only to express my sincere thanks to the Calcutta University for having invited me to deliver these lectures, and to His Highness the Maharaja of Kashmir for having graciously granted permission to avail myself of the invitation.

LECTURE ONE

THE RING FENCE POLICY.

The period which I have chosen as the subject of my lectures is a well defined one in Indian History. It begins with the Regulating Act which was the first direct legislative intervention of Parliament in the affairs of India, and extends to the Mutiny which consummated that intervention by the transfer of the Government of India from the Company to the Crown. In the history of the British Empire in India this period stands out as a definitive and well marked unit. The period of nebulous enterprises and haphazard politics, dominated mainly by considerations of trade, ended with the Regulating Act. The Company stood forth as one of the leading political powers in India, administering territories, negotiating alliances and carrying on wars in the same way and with the same freedom of action towards other States as the leading Indian powers. With the act of 1858 ended the fiction of Government by a Chartered Company, and the Crown of England stood forth as the unquestioned Sovereign of the whole of India from the Himalayas to Cape Comorin.

In 1772 the possessions of the Company were confined to a few scattered settlements along the Coast, the Northern Circars acquired on lease from the Nizam, and the provinces of Bengal, Bihar and Orissa. The whole of North India except the Punjab was under the effective sway of the Marathas who had recovered with surprising rapidity from the disaster which overtook their arms on the fatal field of Panipat. The successors of Asaf Jah, weakened by internal dissensions and external aggression, maintained a precarious hold in the Deccan. In the South, the new Musalman kingdom of Mysore under Hyder Ali established a military sway which was the terror of its neighbours. The Company before 1772 was no match for any of these Powers. Their forces were scattered ; their authority was divided and the material resources at their disposal were not such as to warrant any general plans of conquest. In 1858, the position is changed beyond recognition. The Maratha power had vanished, the descendant of the last of the Peishwas being a homeless wanderer in the unhealthy terais of Nepal. The only remnants of a once glorious empire which bade fair to take on itself the mantle of the Great Moghul were the protected States of Gwalior, Indore, Baroda and Kolhapur. The descendants of Nizam ul Mulk still ruled in Hyderabad, but no longer with the pretensions of derived Moghul authority but as subordinate allies of an all powerful British Government. The dynasty of Hyder Ali was represented by an inoffensive nobleman living under political surveillance in Calcutta. In fine the rivals of the Company had vanished and their place was taken by the present Indian States acknowledging the paramountcy of and in subordinate alliance with the British Crown. A careful observer could have noticed even in 1772 the beginnings of this policy. In fact two partially protected States were in existence even at that time. They were the States of Oudh and the Carnatic. It is important to realise the position in these two States to understand the evolution of British policy in the period that we are dealing with.

At the death of Nawab Dost Ali, the Governor of the Carnatic under Asaf Jah, the French under Benoit Dumas began to interfere in the question of succession. But Asaf Jah had his way and appointed Anwardin to the post. On the death of Asaf Jah resulting in dissensions in the Nizam's family the question of Carnatic succession again came to the forefront. Anwardin was defeated and killed in the battle of Ambur in 1749. The English Company, which had so far taken no part in these quarrels, realising the danger to their trade which would follow the establishment of French political power in the courts of Hyderabad and Arcot, decided to take sides in the question of succession which rose immediately on the death of Anwardin. The French supported the claims of Chanda Sahib and the British sided with Mohammad Ali who was destined later on to earn undying fame because of his enormous debts which became the theme of Burke's flaming eloquence. The celebrated siege of Arcot, which brought out the military genius of an unknown Shropshire lad who had till then only sat at a desk and added up accounts, decided the fate of the Carnatic. Mohammad Ali was recognised Nawab and was declared to be an ally of the English East India Company—a position which was internationally recognised in the Treaty of Paris which mentioned him by name. The rise of Hyder Ali in Mysore and his invasion of the Carnatic forced the Nawab of Arcot into a helpless dependence on the Madras authorities. His sway which nominally extended from Madras to Cape Comorin was of the weakest kind and more than one district had been given out on *Tanka* (or farm) to the officers of the Company. It should however be remembered that there was at that time no limitation on his external relations or on his military power. He was under the protection of the Company but he was not yet in subordinate alliance.

The position in Oudh was slightly dissimilar. The battle of Buxar shattered the military power of Shuja ud Dowla, the Wazir of Oudh. The British force entered Lucknow but the position of the Company did not permit an immediate annexation because it would have given the merchants at Calcutta an extensive land frontier, away from their base on the sea, which they would have had to defend against the Durranies whose empire then included the Punjab and against the Marathas who held the whole of North India. The result was that the

Company made an alliance with their defeated foe the main clause of which was the following :—

"In case the Dominions of H. H. Shuja ud Dowla at any time hereafter be attacked, the East India Company shall assist him with a part or whole of their forces. In the case of the English Company's forces being employed in His Highness' service the extraordinary expenses of the same to be defrayed by him."

By this clause the Company undertook to defend the Nawab Wazir against aggression thus protecting the frontier of their own province of Bengal. "The defence of the Nawab's possessions from invasion is in fact the defence of ours" said Warren Hastings at a later time. The important point was that the army for this common defence was to be maintained by the Nawab and if the English Company went to his help he was to meet the expenditure. Thus the basic principle of the Oudh alliance was defence of the Company's territory at the expense of the Nawab.

In the period between the Treaty of Buxar and the Regulating Act the power of Oudh greatly diminished. "The Wazir had to come to subsist on British strength entirely" declared Warren Hastings. Shuja ud Dowla recognised the position and on the authority of Warren Hastings we know that he often volunteered to accept the suzerainty of the King of England and to carry on the Government as his feudatory as he was supposed to do for Shah Alam.

But even he was not precluded from conducting his own foreign policy or from committing aggression against his neighbours. In fact Warren Hastings, as we shall see later, was afraid of an alliance between him and the Marathas. Though these two States, Oudh and the Carnatic, were effectively under the authority of the East India Company and their rulers were kept on their thrones by the force of the Company's arms, the attitude of the authorities towards them was not that they were feudatories or vassal chiefs, but independent monarchs as could be judged from the following letter from King George III to Mohammad Ali of Arcot.

"Having thought proper to bestow a high mark of Our approbation on two of Our subjects whose conduct We hope will have rendered them worthy of your esteem, We cannot add to the dignity of conferring these honours on them more than by desiring you will represent Our person upon this solemn occasion, and that you will perform those functions for Us which We always perform ourselves when the circumstances will admit. Our intention being to confer the Order of the Bath, one of Our Most Honourable marks of distinction, on Our trusty and well-beloved Sir John Lindsay, Knight, Commander-in-Chief of Our ships and vessels in the East Indies, and of the Marine forces of Our United Company of Merchants trading to and in those parts and on Our trusty and well-beloved Eyre Coote Esquire, Major General of Our forces in the East

Indies and Commander-in-Chief of all the said Company's military forces there. We have directed the said Sir John Lindsay to deliver to you this letter, with the insignias of the Order, and to learn from you the time when it may be most agreeable to you to perform this ceremony as well as to make known to you the nature and manner of bestowing these honours upon him and the said Eyre Coote and so repeating Our wishes for your felicity We bid you heartily farewell. Given at Our Court at St. James' etc. Yours affectionate friend George Rex."

This was then the position in 1774. The Company had become one of the Indian powers and had under its control the Nawabs of Oudh and Arcot. In regard to these States the rudiments of a policy of subordinate alliance had been laid down, though more effectively in Oudh where the Company had to defend Bengal against the Marathas than in the Carnatic. But so far as the Maratha Empire, Mysore and Hyderabad were concerned the Company before this time was not in a position either to attack them or indeed to resist their determined aggression. This had been clearly proved to the satisfaction of Indian powers by the victorious campaign of Hyder Ali in 1769 when he dictated peace at the very gates of Madras.

The Regulating Act marked a change in the Company's fortunes. It brought under unified control the scattered resources of the British in India. Until then the Governors of Presidencies were independent of one another and their policies often conflicted. Each Presidency went its own way, entered into alliances, declared wars and made treaties. The resources of one province were not available in another in times of crises. The creation of a Governor-Generalship at Fort William with general supervisory authority over the other Presidencies was a reform of first rate importance and may be said to be the first stone laid in raising the structure of an imperial Government in India. The emphasis laid on the administrative and political aspect of the Company's activities by Parliament in this Act was also important inasmuch as it relegated to the background the trading operations of the Company which till this time had kept the position of pre-eminence in its councils.

It is not necessary for me to discuss the other provisions of the Regulating Act as they are well-known to all students of Indian History. This much however may be added here that the establishment of a council of equals and the appointment of politicians of the standing of Sir Philip Francis to it, whatever the immediate results they produced, were part of the policy of transforming the Company from a trading corporation into a Government.

The leading powers in India did not realise the change in the position of the Company : in fact none of them except the wily Nawab of Arcot had any knowledge of the political condition in England. They still looked upon the Company as one among themselves, a provincial authority deriving its title from the grant of the Dewani by the Moghul Emperor. So far as they were concerned this was the only title by which the Company held their territorial possessions in Bengal. The might and resources of the British nation which ranged itself behind the Company by the Regulating Act was a factor unknown to them. The interference of Parliament in the affairs of the Company which Lord North, taking advantage of the appeal for a loan from the Directors at Leadenhall Street and the threatened bankruptcy of the Company's finances initiated, though actuated by no friendly considerations, became the very backbone of the Company's strength in India. The ultimate responsibility for the affairs of the Company was taken by Parliament which appointed the Governor General, laid down the lines of policy and kept a watchful eye on the activities of their Agents in India. This was deeply resented by the Directors of the Company as well as by its officials in India. But it is well to recognise that it is the unflinching support of the British Government at crucial moments that gave the Company its strength to meet and defeat the Indian powers and gradually to build up an empire which embraced the whole of India.

Under the Regulating Act Hastings took charge as Governor-General on the 20th October 1774. The prestige of the Company did not stand high at the time. Hyder Ali had dictated peace at the gates of the Company's southern capital. Indian Rulers knew that the finances of the Company were not in a very prosperous condition. The tribute which they had agreed to pay to the Moghul Emperor had not been paid, though repeated demands had been made by Shah Alam. The provinces of Kora and Allahabad which had been given to the Moghul Emperor for his maintenance had been ceded by him to the Marathas, bringing that dreaded people nearer to the Company's frontier. Hastings' first object was to render any attack on the Company's possessions by the Marathas impossible. With this object he returned to Shuja ud Dowla the provinces of Kora and Allahabad hoping thereby that the conflicting claims of the Wazir and the Marathas would render any alliance between them impossible. Hastings did not conceal his motives. He writes thus to his masters in England in a letter dated 4th October 1773 :—

"By ceding them to the Vizier we strengthen our alliance with him, we make him more dependent on us, as he is more exposed to the hostilities of the Marathas we render a junction between him and them which has sometime been apprehended, morally impossible, since their pretensions to Kora will be a constant source of animosity between them."

In 1774 Hastings undertook the war against the Rohillas. We need not, for our purpose, enquire into the justice or otherwise of this wellknown transaction. From the point of view of Hastings' policy towards the States, the Rohilla War is important. Its object was two-fold: (1) to bring Oudh more under the control of the Company and (2) to give the Wazir's dominions a natural boundary which it would be easier to defend. The latter consideration is thus explained by Hastings in a letter to Col. Campion dated 28th May 1774:—

"We engaged to assist the Vizier in reducing the Rohilla country under his dominion that the boundary of his possessions might be completed by the Ganges forming a barrier to cover them from the attacks and insults to which they were exposed by his enemies either possessing or having access to Rohilla country. Thus our alliance with him and the necessity for maintaining this alliance so long as he or his successors shall deserve this protection, was rendered advantageous to the Company's interest, because the security of his possession from invasions in that quarter is in fact the security of ours."

The same consideration of defence led Hastings to guarantee the principality of Benares to Chet Singh. Though Balwant Singh the father of Chet Singh had died in 1770, Shuja ud Dowla had not recognised Chet Singh's succession to the *gadi*. Benares was important strategically to the Company as its possession gave the key to their province of Bihar. Hastings visited Benares in 1773 and himself witnessed the agreement between Shuja ud Dowla and Chet Singh by which the latter was confirmed in his territories on an increased tribute. Writing in 1775 Hastings remarked as follows :—

"The Raja of Benares from the situation of his country which is a frontier of the province of Oudh and Bihar may be made a serviceable ally of the Company whenever their affairs require it. He has always been considered in this light both by the Company and by the successive members of the late Council; but to ensure his attachment to the Company his interests must be connected with it, which cannot be better effected than by freeing him totally from his present vassalage."[1]

In pursuance of this policy Benares was made independent of Oudh and brought directly under the suzerainty of the Company. On the death of Shuja ud Dowla in 1775 the Company made the transfer of Benares a condition of its recognition of Asaf ud Dowla. Article 5 of the Treaty dated 21st May 1775 laid down :—

"The said Nabob for the defence of his country as above specified declares that he has given up of his own free will and accord unto the British Company all districts dependent on the Raja Chet Singh."

The only portion left uncovered in case of a Maratha attack was the side of Midnapur. By the agreement of 1754 Ali Verdi Khan ceded to Raghoji Bhonsla Orissa without Midnapur and thus the Marathas were established on the very borders of

1) Bengal secret consultations—13th February—Report from the Committee of the House of Commons Vol. 5 P. 456 Col: 2.

Bengal. The Marathas demanded *chauth* whenever they felt themselves in a position to exact it and their strong position at Cuttack enabled them to threaten Bengal with greater effect from this side than from any other quarter. The jungle country bordering on Midnapur was however held by the Raja of Mayurbhunj who at the time the Company acquired possession of the area by the grant of Mir Qasim was an adventurous prince by the name of Damodar Bhanja. He was not anxious for the effective extension of Maratha authority into his dominions and was inclined to support the British whenever the Maratha General proposed to attack Bengal. In 1764 Bhawani Pàndit was sent from Nagpur to collect *chauth* from Bengal but the hostility of Damodar Bhanja prevented him from carrying out his intentions. Again in 1768 Sambhuji Pandit became Governor of Orissa and he immediately wrote to the Raja asking him to help in the expedition against Bengal. The English Company realised the strategical importance of Mayurbhunj and Mr. Vansitart in his letter to the Governor stated, "His (Damodar Bhanja's) country is so advantageously situated that with a very little assistance from us he would at any time be able to prevent the Marattas from entering into Bengal from the Southward."[1]

These transactions clearly indicate the policy which under Hastings the Company was evolving.

1) Midnapur Records 11, No. 366.

That has been described rather epigrammatically as the Ring Fence system. The fundamental idea of this system I have described elsewhere as the defence of your neighbour's frontier, of course at his expense, in order to protect your territories. The Company's territories in Bengal were open to attack mainly from the side of Oudh and Benares and Orissa. The Company undertook to help Oudh in protecting its frontiers and also took Benares under its wings. It gave the Company two clear advantages which are described as follows by Hastings himself :—

"We are no longer under the necessity of exhausting the wealth of our provinces in the pay and disbursements of our brigadiers employed at a distance beyond them, but by fixing the sum to be paid by the Vizier for their service and their whole expense and by removing every possible cause for their passing our borders but at his requisition and for his defence we provide effectively for the protection of our frontier and reduce the expenses of the Army even when employing it.

"Besides this object the seat of war in consequence of this alliance was removed from the Company's provinces to those of the Nawab if such supposed war should have been reduced to the defensive."[1]

There was a third result : and that was the virtual reduction of the rulers thus allied to the position of vassals. Both Oudh and Benares are examples of

1) Letter to the Board 4th October 1773.

this. The internal sovereignty of Oudh, though left to the Nawab, soon passed to the Company. Succession to the *gadi* of Lucknow became dependent on the recognition of the Company's authorities at Calcutta and so early as 1775, hardly 10 years after the original treaty, the Company exacted a heavy price for the recognition of Asaf ud Dowla as successor to Shuja ud Dowla. A wide liberty of interference was conceded to the Resident and Oudh was practically converted into a province over which the supreme authority was that of the Company but for whose administration the Company refused to be responsible. Undue intervention by the Residents had become a habit and Hastings had to write to his Agent, Mr. Bristow, not to intervene to settle for the Nawab Wazir "the number of horses which he should be allowed to use and the dishes which should be cooked for his table."

In Benares matters went further. The Raja was actually imprisoned on professing inability to pay a very heavy demand which was made contrary to the agreement of July 5, 1775, in which it was expressly laid down that while he paid his contribution "no demands shall be made on him by the Honourable Company of any kind or any pretence whatsoever, nor shall any person be allowed to interfere with his authority or to disturb the peace of his country."[1]

1) Selection from the letters, despatches and other State papers in the Foreign Deptt. of the Government of India—1772-1785, Vol. II P. 602.

This policy of the Ring Fence implied that the rest of India was foreign territory. It was to defend the Company's possessions from the Marathas that these elaborate precautions were taken. Though so far as the Carnatic, Oudh and Benares were concerned the Company had assumed certain claims of suzerainty, the authorities at Calcutta, Madras and Bombay looked upon the other powers of India as being foreign, and therefore a possible menace to their safety. The Company had just acquired political rights and a position of authority. The Indian powers, especially the Marathas and Hyder Ali, looked upon them as intruders. The wars in the time of Hastings were all waged not with a view to aggrandize the Company's position but solely for the purpose of establishing its claim to equality with other Indian States. The Maratha war and the war with Hyder Ali are of importance only in the sense that at the end of these campaigns the Company came out with their position in India established more firmly than ever. True, they were put to very hard straits. Their finances were ruined beyond repair. Their arms did not meet with any great success. Neither in Madras nor in Bombay were the Company's armies able to force an issue. On the other hand the basis of the Company's power had stood the test well. Not all the power of the Maratha Empire could shake the hold of the Company on Bombay or on Surat. The military genius of Hyder Ali could only lay waste the plains of the

Carnatic but was unable to repeat the performance of 1768. Even the marvellous if ephemeral achievements of Admiral Sufferen, the greatest naval officer that France ever produced, could only shake but not destroy the naval power which was the basis of the Company's unity of action. In 1785 when Hastings surrendered the reins of administration, the British possessions in India had not been increased, but the Company had established its claim to be considered one of the leading powers in India. Its prestige had greatly increased. The Nawab of the Carnatic had entered into a military alliance in 1784 and the Company now stood forth as the only serious rival of the Marathas for the empire of Hindustan. More, by its diplomatic skill it had broken every combination formed against it, and had by establishing special relations with Mahdaji Scindia struck a blow against the central power of the Maratha confederacy from which it never recovered. Warren Hastings, as he himself in a rather pompous minute remarks, had raised and equipped armies, fought against the Marathas, Hyder Ali and the French at the same time, effectively utilised the resources of Oudh and Benares and established in the space of 9 years an empire where only a trading corporation had existed.

There is one further point in the regime of Hastings which remains to be considered and that is his attitude towards the Marathas.

Hastings realised that the real rivals of the British India were the Marathas. He was also convinced that in his time the advantages of strength lay on the side of the Marathas. The war of 1776-82 had proved to him that the position of the Marathas was unassailable. But he recognised the weakness of the loose confederacy in which the Marathas were organised, and his policy was all along to separate from the confederacy Mahdaji Scindia whose ambition of independent dominion he understood but whose loyalty to the central government he under-estimated.

Scindia's object in putting himself forward as the mediator between the British and the Marathas was not so much to establish his independent authority, though no doubt less intervention from Poona would have been welcome, but mainly with a view to establish his position more securely against his rival, Nana Farnavis, and to increase his prestige in the councils of his nation. But the recognition of Scindia as a semi-independent prince directly in contact with the British Company was a point gained by Hastings.

The position at the end of Hastings' regime may be summed up as follows. So far as the general politics of India was concerned the policy of the Ring Fence was well-established. Within that Fence were enclosed Oudh, Benares and the Carnatic. Oudh and the Carnatic though nominally independent were effectively brought under the political control of the Company, the Nawab Vazier being reduced to a nominal authority over his dominions and the Ruler of the Carnatic caught up in the net of private loans from the Company's officers. Hyder Ali, the Marathas and the Nizam were independent powers whose general attitude towards the Company at the beginning of Hastings' rule was not one of respect and confidence. At the end of Hastings' long period of Government the Company's name was respected, though the suspicion of its motives and hostility to its policy continued unabated.

LECTURE TWO

SUBSIDIARY ALLIANCE.

The administration of Hastings became a matter of sensational party conflict culminating in the impeachment of the Governor-General. There were many acts of the Governor-General which were justly open to attack, his war against the Rohillas, his treatment of Chet Singh, the affair of the Begums of Oudh, among others. The interest that was aroused by the administration of Hastings reacted on the general attitude of Parliament towards India. The result was that Pitt's India Act of 1784 contained a preamble which was a notable declaration of policy with regard to Indian States. It said, "And whereas to pursue schemes of conquest and extension of dominion in India are measures repugnant to the wish, the honour and the policy of this nation, be it therefore further enacted that it shall not be lawful for the Governor-General and Council, without the express command of the Court of Directors or the Secret Committee, in any case (except where hostilities have actually been commenced or preparations actually made for the commencement of hostilities against the British nation in India, or against some of the Princes or States whose territories the Company shall be engaged by any subsisting treaty to defend or guarantee) either to declare war or commence hostilities or entering into any treaty for making war, against any of the country Princes or States, in India, or any treaty for guaranteeing the possessions of any country, Princes or States . . . . and in all cases where hostilities shall be commenced or treaty made the Governor-General and Council shall, by the most expeditious means they can devise, communicate the same unto the Court of Directors, together with a full statement of the information upon which they shall have commenced such hostilities, or made such treaties and their motives and reasons for the same at large."

This declaration was meant to prevent the Company from entering into aggressive wars. To carry out this policy the British Government sent out Lord Cornwallis, a peer of Irish lineage who had so far been known mainly for his failures. The personal character of Lord Cornwallis was such that the most disastrous failures could not tarnish his reputation. He had surrendered York Town and thus rendered the British cause in America hopeless : but no one ever accused him of lack of courage. In his long and distinguished career there were at least two such disastrous failures, but whenever there was an appointment which required courage and honesty of purpose he was always chosen. He was sent to carry out the new policy in India. As Viceroy for Ireland he was sent out to settle a problem which had defied British statesmanship for centuries; more, he was sent to negotiate with no less a man than Napoleon the terms of Treaty of Amiens. Again he was sent out to liquidate the heritage of Wellesley's régime. In none of these was his work marked by any distinct achievement, but all the same it was recognised that there was no servant of the Crown more conscientious in the discharge of his duties, none more scrupulous or of more upright or honourable character.

In India he was asked to carry out a policy of neutrality in political affairs and to this he strictly adhered. The third Mysore war which he was forced to declare against Tipu Sultan was covered by the proviso in the Parliamentary enactment, as Tipu had actually attacked the Raja of Travancore who had a treaty of alliance with the Company. It is significant to note that Cornwallis who led the Company's forces himself as Commander-in-Chief did not consider the British forces sufficiently strong to attack Tipu single-handed. He negotiated what he pompously called a Triple Alliance, consisting of the Marathas, the Nizam and the Company. The campaign was fairly successful but not to the extent the Governor-General had hoped. The power of Mysore was weakened, a large indemnity was forced on Tipu and hostages were taken from him for the fulfilment of his obligations. This was the only war that the Company undertook and to that extent the injunction of Parliament was carried out both in letter and in spirit by the Governor-General.

The Mysore war and the policy of the Triple Alliance are important in two ways. It was the first time that the Company definitely added to its territories by conquest. So far the title of the Company to every inch of territory it possessed in India was derived from the grant of some Indian ruler, with the single exception of Bombay; Bengal, Bihar and Orissa from the Moghul Emperor, Northern Circars from the Nizam and the lands attached to various factories from local rulers. The annexation of the districts of the West Coast after the third Mysore war was a significant change of policy, as it was an unequivocal assertion of political sovereignty of the Company and of its position as one among the Indian powers.

Secondly, the policy of the Triple Alliance was the affirmation of the view that the only way of maintaining the peace of India was by an alliance of the principal military powers, the Marathas, the Nizam and the Company. Though designed originally against Tipu, the idea of Cornwallis was that it should be continued on a permanent basis as a guarantee of peace in India.

The attitude of Cornwallis towards Oudh and the Carnatic was entirely different from this. The Parliamentary prohibition was only against new entanglements. In his relations with the Carnatic and Oudh which were both within what may be called the Company's sphere of influence and where a policy of interference had developed, Lord

Cornwallis pressed to the best advantage the position gained by the treaties of Hastings and he himself negotiated new treaties which further weakened the powers of those Rulers. In the Carnatic he forced Mohammad Ali to vest in the Company the sole authority for the defence of his dominion. Shore tried to improve on this at the time Mohammad Ali died (1795) and was succeeded by his son Omdut ul Omrah. So far as Oudh was concerned Shore even went to the extent of openly stating that it was, "both in the opinion of the natives as well as externally, considered a dependency on the British" whatever its relations under the treaties might be.

The engagement of 1788 by which Cornwallis agreed not to make any further demand was violated by Shore who got the Wazir to engage an additional body of troops. Further interference of a more questionable kind followed on the death of Asaf ud Dowla, when after recognizing Wazir Ali as the ruler, Shore put up the claims of Sadat Ali with whom he entered into an agreement for the increase of the Oudh contingent as a price of being installed on the *gadi.*

It would therefore be seen that the policy of non-intervention which Cornwallis followed is altogether different from the policy later known by the same name. As these two policies are often confused it may be desirable to distinguish them clearly and state their points of differences. The policy of non-intervention laid down by Parliament in the Act of 1784 was a prohibition to intervene in the affairs of independent States: it had no bearing on the policy to be followed towards States under the Company's protection. It laid down in express terms that the policy of the Company was not to aggrandise its territory and therefore campaigns of conquest were repugnant to the British people. It was the enunciation of what would now be called a close frontier policy. The Governor-General and Council were asked not to take up an aggressive attitude towards the Marathas, Mysore, Nizam and other States not already in treaty alliance. As the States in treaty alliance with the Company are specially mentioned as worthy of protection even at the cost of wars, it is clear that they were excluded from the operation of this provision. As we have seen, both Cornwallis and Shore, the two statesmen who steadfastly adhered to the so-called policy of non-intervention, did not hesitate to intervene at every turn in the affairs of Oudh and the Carnatic.

The policy of non-intervention as understood at a later time meant that the supreme Government should intervene as little as possible in the internal affairs of protected States, that the autonomy and authority guaranteed to these States by their treaties should not be interfered with, and that their Rulers should be given complete freedom to administer their States in the manner they chose.

During the administration of Cornwallis, the

Marathas and the Nizam more than once proffered treaties of alliance mainly with a view to combined action against Tipu. But Cornwallis who was loyal to his principles refused the alliance till the attack on Travancore by the Mysore forces compelled him to open negotiations himself. The alliance with the Nizam was based on a promise contained in an explanatory letter given to Mir Alam in 1789 by which the 6th article of the treaty of 1768 was extended into a stipulation that the forces mentioned therein "shall be furnished whenever the Nizam shall apply for it provided it is not employed against any powers in alliance with the Company." This letter of Lord Cornwallis was declared by Parliament, by a Resolution dated 15th March 1792, to have the full force of a treaty.

In 1795 the Nizam and the Marathas quarrelled, and the Nizam solicited the help of the Company. Sir John Shore was in a difficult position. The alliance of the Company was the chief source of the Nizam's strength. His whole military power was built up on the basis of having to fight the Marathas and it is for this purpose that he paid for the maintenance of a British force. But Sir John argued that the letter of Cornwallis under which the Nizam claimed his help clearly and unequivocally ruled out the use of British military forces against the Marathas as allies of the Company though the Triple Alliance existed now only in name. Shore was certainly right in his interpretation. Moreover the previous negotiations between the Nizam and the Peishwa showed that these powers had mutually conflicting claims against each other. In these circumstances, to take the side of the Nizam merely because he wanted to evade what the Marathas considered to be their just claims would have been an act of unprovoked aggression—another Rohilla war. Nor was it so easy an affair to challenge the Marathas at that time. A prolonged war would certainly have been the result. The Company's position had not been so consolidated nor the power of the Marathas so weakened by internal dissensions as to justify an anticipation that the war would have had a speedy conclusion. Mysore had not yet been conquered and home domains of the Peishwa were not open to attack. It is impossible to read back to 1795 the conditions of 1803 when Nana Farnavis was dead and the Peishwa was committed to the support of British policy. Shore could have taken no other decision and he was amply justified in it by the clause of the treaty with the Nizam.

The result however was that the Nizam's forces were overwhelmed at Kurdla by the Maratha armies, combined for the last time under the flag of the Peishwa.

This policy of neutrality—it is wrong to call it non-intervention—had disastrous repercussions on the Company's prestige in India. The Nizam, its chief and faithful ally, revolted at what he considered the perfidy of the Company and turned to the French to help him and re-organize his forces.

The Marathas became all powerful in the Deccan; and though the death of Mahdaji Scindia deprived them of a strong, resourceful and far-sighted ruler, their military strength never looked so menacing as when Shore left India. Tipu was brooding over his defeat at the hands of Lord Cornwallis and carrying on negotiations with French adventurers and with Zeman Shah in the vain hope of being able to recover his lost possessions. The defensive foreign policy of Cornwallis and Shore had encouraged the powers of India in an attitude of contempt towards the Company.

Shore's successor was cast in a different mould. Earl Mornington, or the Marquess of Wellesley as he came to be known later, was no bureaucrat like Shore, nor a mere aristocratic mediocrity like Cornwallis. Pompous, assertive and opinionated though he was, Wellesley shared with his brother a keen eye for strategic considerations and a profound understanding of military affairs. Besides, he was gifted with a vivid imagination, an arresting personality and a forceful character. He had another quality not unoften found among empire-builders. He was impatient of official control from Leadenhall Street and unscrupulous as to the methods by which he got round its express and explicit orders. His previous political career had not marked him out for any great position of responsibility. A member of the Irish Parliament and friend and admirer of Grattan, he was, it may be said, by his early training, a liberal. But the translation to the Imperial Parliament seems to have worked a change in his sentiments. He took early interest in Indian affairs, becoming member of the Board of Control in 1793. He was first nominated to the Governorship of Madras, but owing to the fact that Cornwallis who had been selected to come out again had to be sent to Ireland, the post became available for him. On arrival in India he found a situation which was menacing enough. The revival of French power in India in the last decade of the 18th century had indeed been remarkable. A formidable Corps d' Armee of 14,000 sepoys under French officers was maintained by the Nizam. A more powerful and better disciplined army under de Boigne and Perron held the territories around Delhi for Dowlat Rao Scindia. Tipu Sultan had sent his ambassadors to the Isle de France and to Paris. The Maratha Court at Poona was also known to be coquetting with French emissaries. Wellesley could not have found more suitable material to work up the anti-French feeling of the Court and the Secret Committee who, like the rest of England, were at that time swept by an anti-Jacobin agitation. He laid it on deep in his despatches and painted in vivid colours the intrigues of the French with Indian powers, especially with Tipu, which threatened in his view the very existence of British power in India.

It is difficult to imagine that Wellesley believed in the picture he painted : but it was sufficient for him that the material lent colour to his view.

Immediately on arrival, Wellesley made up his mind to declare war against Tipu. But neither from the military nor from the diplomatic point of view was the Company ready for such an important undertaking. The Madras army was in a state of total unpreparedness and the Company had no allies on whom it could depend. The immediate necessity was therefore to re-organize the troops at Madras and negotiate suitable alliances. The latter question was not so easy. The Marathas were not in a friendly mood, especially after the death of Mahadaji Scindia. Also the Marathas knew that the fall of the Mysore kingdom and its inclusion in the British system would spell their own doom. Through Mysore the home territory of the Marathas was open to attack. Once the obstruction of the Mysore power was removed nothing stood in the way of a direct attack on the Maratha territories. An active alliance with the Marathas was therefore impossible. In the case of the Nizam the position appeared to be more serious. The Nizam did not conceal his hostility to a "friend" who had abandoned him in the time of his need. His army was under the control of French officers who would not allow it to be used in British interests. But Wellesley recognised that unless the neutrality of the Marathas could be bought and an active alliance established with the Nizam, there was no possibility of immediate success in a campaign against Mysore. So, Captain Achilles Kirkpatrick, known in Hyderabad as Hashmut Jung, was instructed to offer a permanent treaty of alliance to the Nizam and to see that the French troops were disbanded. The Resident who had accepted the style of living of a Mussalman nobleman and had contracted a local marriage in the *Nika* form, was an adept in the intrigues of the Court. He secured the services of Azim ul Omrah, the Nizam's Prime Minister, and with his help the treaty was negotiated and signed. This treaty enlarged the subsidiary force to 6 battalions on an annual subsidy of Rs. 26,17,100. The Nizam also agreed to disband the troops which were under French command. By a masterful *coup d'etat* the French Corps d' Armee was forced to disband without even a blow being struck. The Nizam's troops passed under British control and he himself ceased to be an independent ruler.

More than all his other achievements Lord Wellesley esteemed this subsidiary alliance which he negotiated with Hyderabad. In his official portrait which hangs in the Council Chamber in the city of Calcutta, he is seen holding a paper bearing the legend : Subsidiary Treaty, Hyderabad, 1798. It is also significant that the annuity of £5,000 that was granted to him by the Court of Directors was to date from the signature of this treaty by the Nizam. Nor is this judgment which ranks the Treaty of

Hyderabad above the capture of Seringapatam or the battle of Assaye, in any sense wrong. It is the treaty of Hyderabad that is the bed rock of Indian State policy and the foundation on which the Imperial edifice of Britain in India has been built. As the fundamental principles of Indian State policy are enshrined, so to say, in this treaty, its main and distinguishing characteristics may be analysed here. These were three:

1. It was indissoluble. After the signature of this treaty the Nizam was not free to pick and choose his friends. The State came to be in 'permanent alliance' with the British.

2. There was a British Army officered by Europeans but paid for by the Nizam established in his territory. This force was for the purpose of internal as well as external defence and it gave to the Company a handle wherewith to influence the internal affairs of the State.

3. The treaty stipulated that the foreign relations of the Nizam should be conducted exclusively through the Company.

These three characteristics were, as we have pointed out, developed slowly during the 50 years of relations with Oudh and Arcot. The subsidiary system did not come suddenly into existence like some mythical monster with all its characteristics fully developed. With the increasing power of the East India Company, new restrictive clauses were introduced to the original stipulation of a subsidiary force to be paid for by the Ruler. It is in the Hyderabad treaty that we meet with all these clauses in their fully developed form. The Hyderabad treaty may therefore be said to be the subsidiary treaty *par excellence* and the consequence that followed from the special characteristics noted above may therefore be analysed.

First, it may be said here that the East India Company did not in any way conceal their object in negotiating the Hyderabad treaty. "The fundamental principles of His Excellency the Governor-General's policy in establishing the subsidiary alliance is to place the States in such a degree of dependence on the British power as may deprive them of the means of prosecuting any measure hazardous to the security of the British Empire."[1]

The permanent and indissoluble character of the alliance made the Ruler a subordinate and unequal ally. Though the Nizam realised that in allowing the Marathas to be crushed, he was sealing his own doom, the treaty gave him no loophole as his own forces were under the effective command of the British Resident. The permanent nature of the alliance also tended to give the executive decisions of the British Government the forces of finality, as there was no method of settlement by arbitration or otherwise of questions on which there was divergence of opinion.

1) Despatches of the Government of India to the Resident at Hyderabad, 4th February, 1804.

5

The second feature, the establishment of a subsidised force within the territory of the Ruler, was even more pregnant with disastrous consequence for the State. A subsidised force meant an army kept within the allied State by the British Government for the expenses of which a subsidy was given by the protected ruler.

It was usually postulated that the subsidy (which formed generally about one-third of the revenue of the State) should be paid annually. The Company's Government knew well enough that so heavy a demand on States' revenues could not easily be met with any regularity especially in India where revenues shrink or expand according to the monsoon. The result was, as the Duke of Wellington foresaw, that the States fell into arrears. This gave the Company opportunity to annex the most valuable portions of the territory of its allies. The principle on which the commutation of subsidy was generally negotiated is put in the following words by the Marquis of Wellesley himself in a Despatch to the Secret Committee of the Board of Control in advising the Court of Directors to follow the Hyderabad precedent in the Oudh negotiations. Wellesley stated "In commutation of 40 lakhs a country rated at the annual value of 62 lakhs of rupees was taken away in full sovereignty in the Nizam's case."[1]

The pay and allowances of the Nizam's contingent officered by the British but paid for by the Hyderabad

1) Wellesley's despatches, p. 205.

State were many times more than what prevailed in the Company's forces or in the British Army. The Commandant was paid £5,000 a year and the other officers were paid in proportion. The object of this contingent was thus explained[1] with refreshing candour by the Government of India at a later time :—

"When for *our private views that prince was constrained to support a body of our troops to be stationed near his capital* the then Government disguised the *interested oppressiveness* by the sturdy declaration that His Highness had spontaneously sought the aid of a subsidiary force to secure his person and territories."[2]

The subsidiary force besides dislocating the finances and demoralising the administration also gave the Company the pretext for internal interference. Wellesley enunciated this principle in relation to Oudh. As the Nawab's "authority is upheld by the terror of our name and exercised by the immediate force of our arms" and as the Nawab himself is "sustained exclusively by his connection with the Company's Government and the reputation and honour of the British nation" the Governor-General claimed that the right to interfere in any matter whatsoever rested with the Company.[3] This principle in the form that Wellesley enunciated was

1) Kaye's life of Metcalfe, p. 15, Vol. II.
2) Bengal Political Letter, 20th December 1822 (Government of India to Metcalfe).
3) Wellesley's despatches, p. 209.

capable of application to every case of a subsidiary alliance.

The third characteristic was the stipulation that the State in subsidiary alliance should have no foreign relations. It was only in 1784 that this clause was introduced in the treaty with the Nawab of Arcot. But with no other State had the Company so far insisted upon this restriction. In the treaty with the Nizam, Wellesley introduced it as an essential feature of subsidiary alliance because his policy from the beginning was to isolate the Marathas and make any alliance between the Deccan powers impossible.

Though with the Hyderabad treaty the subsidiary alliance in all its essential features came into existence and all the problems of internal intervention, restriction of sovereign powers, forced appointment of Dewans and control of succession began to agitate Anglo-Indian statesmen even at the beginning of the century, it should not be thought that a political system embracing the whole of India was brought into being at the time. Such no doubt was Wellesley's idea. But he was successful only with the Peishwa and with the Nizam. The treaty with Scindia in 1804 left him a sovereign power whose independence was acknowledged. The treaty with Holkar was also not of the kind which reduced him to the position of a subordinate ally. In 1809 Lord Minto refused to enter into an alliance with Bhopal. By the agreement negotiated by Minto after the departure of Wellesley and the death of Cornwallis who was sent out to replace him, the commitments in Central India were reduced and the subsidiary alliance of the Company even dissolved in some cases.

There are two considerations with regard to the relations of the Company with the Indian powers at this time to which it is necessary to direct our attention.

All the treaties except that with Mysore are negotiated on a basis of equality. The Company did not claim any paramountcy or authority and the treaties themselves clearly show that at least in the case of those States which were not conquered there was a spirit of reciprocity. As the great Maratha powers and the Nizams were in the enjoyment of absolute internal and external sovereignty, the reciprocity established with them was not merely a verbal formality or something to so, the wounded susceptibilities but a historical fact.

Each of these treaties guarantees in a most absolute manner the absolute authority of the Ruler over his own subjects and most unequivocally repudiate any claim to intervene in the affairs of the State. That the clause so laid down was not merely a friendly profession may be seen from the fact that Wellesley recognised its baneful influence, and where he had the chance, as in Mysore, he was careful enough to omit it.

"Recollecting the inconvenience and embarrassments which have arisen to the parties concerned under the double Governments and conflicting authorities unfortunately established in Oudh, Carnatic and Tanjore, I resolved to reserve for the Company the most extensive and indisputable rights of interposition in the internal affairs of Mysore."[1]

If, after realising the baneful influence of this system of guaranteeing absolute authority, Wellesley and his successors were forced to insert a clause of this kind uniformly in all treaties, it is clear it could not have been done as an act of mere formality.[2]

After Mysore had been conquered and the Nizam brought effectively under the Company's authority, only the Marathas remained as an independent power in India. Wellesley made no secret of his intention of bringing the vast and powerful empire of the Marathas also within his scheme of subsidiary union. Even in 1800 (letter of October 2) after Mysore had been conquered and the Nizam reduced, Wellesley wrote as follows to Lady Anne Barnard:

"I will heap kingdoms upon kingdoms, victory upon victory, revenue upon revenue, I will accumulate glory and wealth and power until the ambition and advice even of my masters shall cry mercy." It is clear from this that even before the treaty of Bassein was signed, Wellesley had made up his mind to fight the Marathas, for after 1800 there was no other nation left from whom to wrest "kingdoms upon kingdoms." With this object in view he offered the Peishwa a

1) Despatch to the Court of Directors, August 3, 1799.

2) This has been taken bodily from a contribution by me to the Annals of the American Academy of Political and Social Science, Vol. cxlv.

subsidiary alliance which that ruler was persuaded by Scindia and Holkar to refuse. Wellesley's idea was that once the Peishwa accepted the subsidiary alliance the other Maratha rulers could be brought to obedience, on the plausible pretext of effectuating of the central authority of Poona over its overgrown feudatories. Wellesley had no illusions about the attitude of the Maratha chiefs to the proffered alliance. But he knew that Baji Rao was unmindful of the interests of the Maratha people. The son of the old pretender Raghoba, through whom the Bombay Government had tried to establish British authority prior to the treaty of Salbai, Baji Rao was by hereditary tradition and by political exigencies a suitable instrument for the effectuation of Wellesley's policy. If he could be persuaded to accept the treaty, the Company could put forward a legal claim to the control of the chieftains nominally subordinate to Poona. Sir George Barlow, the senior member of Council, in his memorandum dated the 8th July 1803, stated this policy in the following terms :—

"It is absolutely necessary that no native State should be left to exist in India which is not upheld by the British power or the political conduct of which is not under its absolute control. The restoration of the head of the Maratha Empire to his Government through the influence of the British power in fact has placed all the remaining States in India in this dependent relation to the British

Government. If the alliance with the Peishwa is maintained, its natural and necessary operation would in course of time reduce Scindia and the Raja of Berar to a state of dependence on the Peishwa and consequently upon the British Government."[1]

Baji Rao signed the treaty of Bassein and accepted British authority in the name of the Maratha State ; but if Wellesley had calculated that he could bring Scindia, Holkar and others under him without striking a blow as he had done in Hyderabad, he was sadly mistaken. The Peishwa had signed, but the Maratha Princes refused to acknowledge the treaty as binding, and a prolonged war was the result. We need not go into any details of the campaign which opened with such a victory for the British arms as the renowned battle of Assaye. It need only be said that the campaign did not go altogether as Wellesley had anticipated. General Monson's retreat before Holkar and Lake's repeated failures at Bharatpur had shaken the prestige of British arms. Neither Scindia nor the Raja of Berar, in spite of spectacular victories over them, had been effectively reduced. Scindia's military power was yet unbroken, and that chief, though he had suffered important reverses, was still in a position to undertake offensive operations. On the other hand, the Company's treasury was empty and the Directors at home were clamouring for a cessation of hostilities. In fact, the Maratha war on

1) Wellesley Despatches, Vol. III, 185.

which Wellesley had entered with the light hearted assurance of a speedy victory which would establish the unquestioned paramountcy of the Company all over India turned out to be more than what the Company's financial and military resources could bear at that time.

The period between the recall of Wellesley and the appointment of the Earl of Moira, better known as the Marquis of Hastings, was a relieving hiatus in the growth of British policy in India. This period offers us an opportunity for a retrospective review of the thirty years we have so far dealt with. In the beginning, as we noticed, the Company was hardly in a position of equality with Indian powers. The wars of Warren Hastings may with justification be called the fight for equality. When Wellesley laid down the reins of Government, the Company though not yet supreme was still the predominant power in India. The Maratha confederacy had been broken diplomatically at Bassein and on the field of battle at Assaye, though Scindia and Holkar continued to be independent.

The Mohammedan power in Mysore had vanished and had come to be considered merely as an unpleasant paranthesis in the long history of the Hindu dynasty of that kingdom which was now recreated as a protected State. The Nizam was transformed by the treaty of 1798 into a subsidiary ally and the Carnatic had been annexed.

What was more important for our purpose than

the political and territorial changes indicated above was the growth of a definite policy towards Indian States as such. We have noticed that in the time of Hastings, the Company had no decided policy with regard to these States except that of using them as the first line defence for the protection of Bengal, Bihar and Orissa. There was no intention of evolving a political system of which these States formed a part. Nana Farnavis himself offered to subsidise a British force in 1790 but his offer was declined.[1]

Wellesley set out not merely to establish the pre-eminent position of the Company by breaking the power of its principal rivals but to evolve a system of Imperial Government reducing such Indian States as had already come under its protection to the position of utter subordination and by bringing into a general system of subsidiary alliance the other States as had so far stood out of the sphere of the Company's influence. So far as the first part of the policy, that of reducing the States already in alliance, was concerned, Wellesley had no difficulty. As we have mentioned before, he was able after the fall of Seringapatam "to reserve the Company the most extensive and indisputable rights of interposition in the internal affairs of Mysore."[2]

In the new treaty which he negotiated with Travancore there was a clause introduced by which

1) Macdonald, Life of Nana Farnavis—Oxford University Press, 1927, p. 82.
2) Despatch of 3rd August, 1799.

the Raja undertook to abide by whatever advice the Resident might offer. Article 9 of the Travancore treaty of 1805 contains the following provision :—

"His Highness hereby promises to pay at all times the utmost attention to such advice as the British Government shall occasionally judge it necessary to offer him with a view to the economy of his finances, the better collection of his revenues, the administration of justice, the extension of commerce, the encouragement of trade, agriculture and industry or any other objects connected with the advancement of His Highness' interests, the happiness of his people and the mutual welfare of both."

By the treaty of 1801 with Oudh, the Governor-General reserved to himself "the positive rights of interference in the internal management of that part of the country retained by the Nawab Vizier."[1] After the conquest of Mysore, the Carnatic was annexed. Thus all the old allies of the Company were converted into actual dependents. So, this part of Wellesley's policy met with unqualified success.

The next step in the policy was to bring the other major powers into the system of subsidiary alliance. With the Nizam, as we have seen, he was able to conclude a treaty on this basis. Only the Marathas remained, and Wellesley got Baji Rao to sign the treaty of Bassein, though the leading Maratha Chiefs

1) Despatch of the Secret Committee dated 14th November, 1801.

had expressed themselves openly against it. The treaty of Bassein was signed, but as we have seen Wellesley had to contend not only against a weak and vacillating Baji Rao but against Jaswant Rao Holkar, the Raja of Nagpur and the armies of Scindia. The power of resistance which the Marathas showed at this crisis deprived Wellesley of the satisfaction of uniting the whole of India under the Company's authority and thus earning for himself a Dukedom and the Garter which he had not hesitated to ask of the Cabinet as a reward for his victory over Tipu.

The Court of Directors after long murmurings finally asserted their authority against Wellesley's grandiose schemes of aggrandisement and recalled him in August 1805. Lord Cornwallis was sent out again with definite instructions to withdraw from the commitments and liabilities which Wellesley's forward policy towards the Marathas had forced on the Company. Before Cornwallis could put into force the views of the Court, he died and was succeeded by Sir George Barlow.

The immediate effect of this reversal of policy was the withdrawal from the proposed subordinate alliances with the Maratha Chiefs. The Company even undertook not to make any treaties with States over which the Marathas had a claim. This was with special reference to the States of Rajputana which were left to be dealt with by Scindia and Holkar. The timely arrival of Cornwallis postponed the negotiation of alliance with Rajput States, and the assertion of British supremacy over the Maratha States. Lord Minto, who followed Barlow, continued the policy of Cornwallis and avoided entangling alliances, but the unsettled condition of Bundelkhand and Kathiawad where the sovereignty of the Peishwa had ceased to be effective, forced him to make a temporary settlement with the Chiefs of these areas by which the British Government guaranteed their position and status. The expanding power of Ranjit Singh in the Punjab and the possibility of his bringing together under him the whole of the Sikh nation also compelled the Governor-General to take the Cis-Sutlej States under the military protection of the Company.

It was however clear to all that this system by which the Company withdrew unto itself could not last long. The Anglo-Indian officials who carried out the policy of the Governor-General were openly out of sympathy with what they called the mean and unimaginative policy of the commercial magnates of Leadenhall street, who looked more to the profits of their concern and to the value of East India stock than to a forward policy "which annually calls for re-inforcement of men and for remittances of money and which yields little other profits except brilliant gazettes." Metcalfe described the policy of "non-intervention" as "monstrous," and this was the general opinion of the political officers who had already begun to see in imagination the map of India painted wholly red. These diplomatists and statesmen found in the Marquis of Hastings who succeeded Lord Minto as Earl Moira an avowed champion of their views.

LECTURE THREE

THE POLICY OF ANNEXATION

The Marquis of Hastings gathered up the threads of Wellesley's policy and brought under effective British supremacy the whole of India, east of the Sutlej and the Indus. His wars and campaigns may be studied from any standard history of India. For our purpose it is sufficient to discuss the principles of his settlement, the policy he followed in the new alliances he contracted and the general course of his relationship with the States already under the Company's protection. By his successful operations against the Pindarees he brought central India under effective occupation. With the defeat of Holkar's army at Mehdipur, Indore came under the paramountcy of the Company.

On the 13th of June 1817, a treaty was negotiated with the Peishwa under Article IV of which Baji Rao gave his consent "for himself and for his heirs and successors, to the dissolution in form and substance of the Maratha confederacy and renounced all connection whatever with other Maratha powers whether arising from his former situation of executive head of the Maratha Empire or from any other cause." After the battle of Kirkee the Peishwa's dominions were annexed to form the major portion of the Bombay Presidency. The Rajput States were taken under protection and treaties were negotiated with them. By these operations the scheme on which Wellesley entered when he negotiated the treaty of Bassein was brought to completion.

The following are the important treaties negotiated by Hastings :—

State	Year
Kutch	1817
Karanti	1817
Samthar	1817
Bhopal	1817
Kotah	1817
Jodhpur	1818
Mewar	1818
Bundi	1818
Bikaner	1818
Kishangarh	1818
Jaipur	1818
Pratapgarh	1818
Dewas	1818
Jaisalmer	1818
Banswara	1818
Dhar	1818
Rajpipla	1821

Besides these treaties, the administration of Marquis of Hastings also witnessed the settlement of Kathiawad, Bundelkhand and the Simla Hill States.

The treaties he negotiated with States which came under the protection of the Company are of special interest. The Maratha confederacy had been finally broken at the field of Kirkee and the pre-eminence of the British in India was established beyond dispute. The necessity which Wellesley had felt of securing allies in his campaigns against the power of Marathas had ceased to exist. This change in the position of the Company was reflected in the treaties negotiated by Hastings with the Rajput States. In most of these treaties the rights of protection and the authority of arbitration are explicitly laid down. A new principle of subordinate co-operation is introduced in the treaties in place of the reciprocal obligations of treaties entered into with independent States in the time of Wellesley. Even in regard to the Nawab of Bhopal, whose exertions in "supplying with provisions our columns .... and in contributing eight hundred horses to the division of Lt.-Colonel Adams through the campaign have been so meritorious"[1] that it was impossible to deny him British protection, the clause relating to subordinate co-operation is expressly laid down. It is curious that most of these treaties also lay down that with regard to his internal affairs the Ruler is absolute and that British law will not be introduced within his territories. But the saving provision of subordinate co-operation was capable of indefinite expansion as later history has amply demonstrated.

Lord Hastings' settlement of Bundelkhand and Kathiawad was altogether on a new principle. British authority in both these areas was derived from treaties made at the time of Wellesley, but that Governor-General had not been able to make any

1) E.I.C. Papers on the Pindary Wars, 1824, p. 203.

definitive settlement for their administration. Lord Cornwallis and others who followed him left these States in the same unsettled position of conflicting suzerain authorities. But after the Pindarees had been crushed and the Maratha power destroyed, it was thought desirable to bring these areas under a definite political settlement. So far the Company had negotiated with individual States and entered into treaty alliances with them, guaranteeing them their rights and undertaking obligations towards them. In Bundelkhand which had been ceded in *sovereignty* to the Company, the policy followed was different. The whole of Bundelkhand except Orcha had been under the effective authority of the Marathas. Though the entire area was annexed to the British dominions, as a broad line of settlement the Rulers were continued in their rights and powers. Only 3 States in this area,Orcha, Datia and Samthar, have formal treaties with the British Government. The rest are the outcomes of a political settlement where in consideration of the general conditions of the province, a policy of indirect Government through local Chiefs was enforced as a cheaper and perhaps more effective system. It is only after the Mutiny when the policy of annexation was put a stop to, and every Prince or Chief who had a vestige of jurisdiction left with him raised to the status of a sovereign Ruler, that these areas came to be officially recognised as Indian States.

In Kathiawad the position was slightly different.

Both the Peishwa and the Gaekwar claimed sovereign rights over Kathiawad. By the treaty of 1805 between the Company and the Gaekwar, the former guaranteed his rights over Kathiawad. The Gaekwar was advised to take fixed money payments and leave the Chiefs in full possession of internal autonomy. But the arrangement was only in relation to the Gaekwar's claims. The Peishwa also claimed sovereign authority. By the treaty of 1817 with Baji Rao, the absolute sovereignty over these provinces was conveyed to the Company. (Articles 7 and 13) and thus the authority of the Peishwa became vested in the Company. In 1820 the Gaekwar's rights were by agreement taken over by the Company. The area thus brought under the Company's authority was not annexed as it would have affected the claims of the Gaekwar, and hence the Princes and Chiefs of Kathiawad were continued in their authority, though for a long time it was a matter of controversy whether the area was actually a part of British India like the provinces and districts under the direct administration of the British Empire.

It will be seen from the facts stated above that though an aggressive champion of the policy of extending British authority in India, Hastings was not an annexationist. In the unsettled areas he preferred a policy of maintaining the local Chiefs and Zamindars in authority. The self-complacent view which was later on to gain such vogue under

Auckland, Ellenborough and Dalhousie, that it was the moral duty of the British Government to bring the blessings of civilisation to the subjects of Indian Rulers whenever an opportunity offered for their annexation, was not shared by Hastings who saw in these minor chieftaincies, which he propped up with such laborious care in Bundelkhand, Kathiawad and Simla Hills, powerful support to the British Government for the security of its empire in India. All through the writings of the better known statesmen of the time like Munro, Malcolm and Elphinstone can be detected a fear that some time or other these areas may be brought under direct administration—a possibility which Malcolm at least looked upon with grave misgivings.

Hastings' views with regard to internal intervention in the States allied to the Company were also in consonance with his idea of maintaining the Princes unimpaired in their authority which he pursued to such lengths in Kathiawad and Malwa. To C. T. Metcalfe, Resident at Hyderabad, he wrote as follows in reply to a letter asking for authority to intervene in the affairs of the Nizam :—

"1. Your letters of the 31st August and 3rd and 5th September, have been laid before the Governor-General in Council, and I am directed to communicate the observations which occured on their perusal.

"2. In the second paragraph of your first letter you say that 'you propose our interference in the

Nizam's affairs to be not merely right, but also a duty, arising out of our supremacy in India which imposed on us the obligation of maintaining the tranquillity of all countries connected with us, and consequently of protecting the people from oppressions, as no less necessary than the guaranteeing of their rulers against revolution.' The assumption of our possessing a universal supremacy in India involving such rights as you have described is a mistake. Over States which have by particular engagement rendered themselves professedly feudatory, the British Government does, no doubt, exercise supremacy; but it never has been claimed, and certainly never has been acknowledged, in the case of Native powers standing within the denomination of allies. Although a virtual supremacy may undoubtedly be said to exist in the British Government from the inability of other States to contend with its strength, the making such a superiority a principle singly sufficient for any exertion of our will, would be to misapply and to pervert it to tyrannic purpose.

"3. In your third paragraph you observed 'the only refuge of a people intolerably vexed, is in emigration or insurrection; and as we ensure the Nizam's Government against rebellion, it seems to be incumbent on us to save his subjects from grievous oppressions.' The argument of supremacy having been set aside, nothing but the tenure of some special engagement could render us liable to the call or allot to us the title for such interposition. Our treaties, characterising the Nizam as an independent sovereign, authorise no such latitude. When for our private views that prince was constrained to support a body of our troops to be stationed near his capital, the then Government disguised the interested oppressiveness of making him pay a portion of our army for holding him in thraldom by a sturdy declaration that His Highness had spontaneously sought the aid of a subsidiary force to secure his person and territories. The veil thus thrown over our policy required that any stipulations which could mark the prostration of his power should be forborne so that in appearance he legitimately retained his freedom. The measure however really placed him at our mercy. It was hardly to be imagined that our advantage would not be abused and it was abused; the independence which the very conditions of the compact recognised and pledged us to respect, was set at naught. Gradual but unequivocal encroachments on the Nizam's just authority were perceived by the honourable Court and a more becoming system was enjoined. The Governor-General in Council laboured to introduce it—a work of no small difficulty when the country was so disorganised—and having established an understanding with Raja Chandu Lal for the correction and future conduct of affairs (this Government in return binding itself to support that Minister) the Resident was directed to adopt a course of conciliatory counsel instead of those starts of despotic dictation which had before been in use. That limited degree of interference would still be objectionable but for the common interests between the two Governments, that His Highness' territories should be restored to prosperity; yet even that excuse would be insufficient, were not our influence to be managed with delicacy, and to be unavowed. Such is the distinct nature of our relations with the Nizam; and a disregard of its terms would be no less repugnant to general principles, than to the orders of this Government.

"4. Paragraph 4 and 5 plead necessity for our interposition, because the Nizam does not rule his subjects with equity and prudence. The fact of maladministration is unquestionable and must be deplored. Does that, however, decide the mode in which alteration is to be effected? Where is our right to determine that the amount of the evil is such as to demand our taking the remedy into our hands? His Lordship in Council observes that the necessity stated is altogether constructive. Were such a pretence allowable, a powerful State should never want a colour for subjugating a weak neighbour. The consequence is so obvious that no principle in the law of nations leaves room for acting on such a presumption. It is admitted, that if convulsions rage so violently in one State as clearly to threaten the excitation of ferment in a bordering one, the latter may be justified in reducing to order the nation by which its tranquillity was menaced. This, however, is an extreme case, at the same time that it is of a description strictly defined. No analogy exists between indisputable exigency and an asserted convenience, where vague arbitrary charges, if tolerated as a ground of procedure, would furnish ready pretext for the foulest usurpations."

Again in his private journal dated February 6th, 1816, he writes :—

"Our object ought to be to render the British Government paramount in effect, if not declaredly so. We should hold the other States as vassals, in substance, though not in name ; not precisely as they stood in the Moghul Government but possessed of perfect internal sovereignty and only bound to repay the guarantee and protection of their possessions by the British Government with the pledge of two great feudal duties:

"First, they should support it with all their forces in any call. Second, they should submit their mutual difference to the head of the confederacy (our Government) without attacking each other's territories. A few subordinate stipulations on our part with immunities secured in return to the other side (especially with regard to succession) would render the arrangement ample without complication or undue latitude. Were this made palatable to a few States, as perhaps it easily might, the abrogation of treaties with the powers who refuse to submit to the arrangement would soon work upon their apprehensions in a way that would bring them at last within the pale of the compact. The completion of such a system, which must include the extinction of any pretension to pre-eminence in the court of Delhi, demands time and favourable coincidences. While on the other hand, the difficulties bequeathed to me are imminent, and might break upon me at any instant. A new Government always produces some suspension in animosities. I have endeavoured to improve the juncture by courteous and conciliatory language to the native powers; and do hope I may remove considerable soreness. As for the rest, fortune and opportunities must determine: but it is always well to ascertain to one self what one would precisely desire, had one the means of commanding the issue."

The period of alliance and the creation of Indian States may be said to have practically come to an end with the Marquis of Hastings. The Company had become predominant in India and had displaced the Moghul and the Maratha in the claim of a general supremacy over the peninsula. The Governors-General in the generation that followed were dominated by other considerations and were frankly annexationists in their policy. The only important exception is in the case of Jammu and Kashmir, where Gulab Singh was recognised an independent sovereign in consideration of his attitude at the time of the Sikh troubles. But the period from the retirement of the Marquis of Hastings to the Mutiny is of great importance to Indian States as it witnessed the gradual growth of the authority of the Residents in the matter of internal administration. During this time of administrative developments, the resident ministers of the Company at Indian Courts were slowly but effectively transformed from diplomatic agents representing a foreign power into executive and controlling officers of a superior Government.

Early European diplomacy recognised Resident Political officers as ambassadors of an inferior class. Though it has gone out of usage in Europe it was a common designation in the 18th Century. The author of "le Droit de Gens" says that the position of the Resident is of the same nature as that of the envoy but below in rank. The Congress of Aix la Chappelle (1818) created Ministers-Resident accredited to sovereigns. In India, for special negotiations the Company used in early days to send their envoys or Vakils, but when their political power increased they appointed Resident officers. The Residents to Indian States appointed in the early years of the Company's political power were merely agents to press forward the interests of the Company and watch the policy of the State to which they were accredited—a position similar to that of the Resident in Nepal when the political official at Khatmandu was known by that name. The Court of Directors, in a despatch dated 1st of April, 1772, directed the Bombay Government that a Resident Envoy should be appointed at Poona. The intention was only to remain in friendly association. Mr. Thomas Moyston was appointed to the post but he had no political power whatever. This point about the general position of the Residents was well understood at the time. No claim was made for political power. Even so great a stickler after form as the Marquis of Cornwallis stated : "I expect that all the Princes of the country except those of the Royal family shall habituate themselves to consider the English Residents at their respective courts as the representatives of a government at least equal in power and dignity to their own."[1]

In Oudh, however, where the Company began to exercise certain definite rights, the Resident became soon a controlling officer ; and Warren Hastings as we noticed before had to warn him not to interfere in the matter of the horses in the Wazir's stable and the dishes to be cooked in his kitchen. But everywhere else the Resident was confined to his diplomatic duties. Even rulers like Mahdaje Scindia who were more powerful than the Company at the time, accepted Resident-Ministers at their Court. These officers were not then as they are now the sole channels of communication with the Company, as the States had the right of keeping their resident representatives at Calcutta. By the treaty of Mandasaur in 1818, it was agreed "that an accredited Minister from the British Government shall reside with Maharaja Malhar Rao Holkar and the latter

1) Cornwallis' correspondence, p. 5581

shall be at liberty to send a Vakil to the Most Noble the Governor-General." Other States also had this right, Kashmir in fact enjoying it till 1885.

The powers of the Resident increased with the new treaty concluded with the Nizam. As the object of that treaty was to secure the resources of the Nizam for the fight against Tipu, the Resident was instructed to so shape the policy of the State as to suit the end of the Company. The following incident narrated by Col. Briggs illustrates the authority which the Residents were acquiring at that time :—

"In this year (1804) occured the death of Azeemul Omrah the Prime Minister, when the Nizam was strongly urged by the Resident to nominate Mir Alum to the vacant appointment. The Mir had long been known to be favourably inclined towards the British; and as the Nizam's disposition was sullen and discontented and too fickle to be relied on, it was rightly urged that any advantage to be derived by the British from an alliance with the Hyderabad State depended in placing its resources under the control of a minister who should owe his elevation exclusively to their influence."

Mir Alum was thus appointed Prime Minister but there was a strong party against him at Court. In order to support the minister who had thus been forced on the Nizam, the Resident had naturally to intervene decisively in all matters. The action taken by the Resident in order to get rid of all opposition to his creature best explains the situation.

Mir Alum, on the present pretext of paying a visit of condolence to the Resident, took shelter in the Residency when the latter compelled the Nizam to dismiss the opposition leaders, Ismail Yar Jung and Raja Mohiput Ram, from his Court. Thereafter the Minister returned to the city and took up his office as Prime Minister of the sovereign whom he had deserted, and even asked that a force should be detached for the protection of his person. After Mir Alum's death, the Resident procured the appointment of another of his nominees, Munir ul Mulk. "The real though not avowed object," says Colonel Briggs, "of the British Resident through these negotiations was to effect an arrangement which, while it gave to the Nizam the appearance of having exercised his prerogative of appointing his own Dewan, *left the executive* in the hands of a minister who should be indebted to the Resident alone for his elevation to power and feel that his maintenance in office depended solely on his subserviency to his wishes."[1] Matters went so far in the Nizam's Court that when during the administration of Chandu Lal, who took his orders from the Residency, the Nizam desired to ask him to furnish certain accounts, the Resident, Mr. Russel, considered it 'undue interference' in the duties of the minister.

The Resident's powers soon began to increase with the claim to give 'advice' to Rulers. In the

1(Brigg's Nizam, p. 95.

treaty with Travancore negotiated in 1805, it was laid down that the Maharaja would accept any advice given by the paramount power in all matters of importance. This gave the Resident not merely the right to be consulted but invested his opinions with the authority of an executive order which the Ruler had perforce to obey. Even in the case of States which were not obliged by treaty to accept such advice, the Government of India interpreted the agreement of the Rulers to act in subordinate co-operation to mean that when any advice was given it will be implicitly followed.

The extent to which the Resident's power had been aggrandised may be seen from the fact that Col. Macaulay wrote to the Raja of Cochin as follows: "The Resident will be glad to learn that on his arrival near Cochin the Raja will find it convenient to wait upon him."[1]

By these unseen processes the powers of the Resident were so aggrandised during the period following the establishment of British paramountcy after Lord Hastings that by Lord Dalhousie's time the Residents became virtually the rulers of the State. They became the sole channels of communication with the British Government and their authority pervaded every branch of State administration. The evil was seen and realised early by farseeing political officers like Malcolm who strongly condemned this tendency. Sir Charles Metcalfe,

1) Cochin State Manual, p. 138.

another very distinguished political officer, declared that 'an interfering agent is a nuisance wherever he may be, and our agents are apt to take that turn.'

In his private journal dated February 1, 1814, the Marquis of Hastings wrote :—

"In our treaties with them (Indian Princes) we recognise them as independent sovereigns. Then we send a Resident to their Courts. Instead of acting in the character of ambassador, he assumes the functions of a dictator ; interferes in all their private concerns ; countenances refractory subjects against them, and makes the most ostentatious exhibition of this exercise of authority. To secure himself the support of our Government, he urges some interest which, under the colour thrown upon it by him, is strenuously taken up by our Council ; and the Government identifies itself with the Resident not only on the single point but on the whole tenor of his conduct."

The acceptance of a Resident was understood by Indian States to mean their complete subordination. As a result, Gulab Singh who had seen the system working in other States refused to entertain a Resident, and though the proposal to appoint a political officer in Kashmir was pressed on him, he refused to yield and carried his point.

Though such interference on the part of the paramount power had become the normal course, the Government of India had not yet realised that the claim of paramountcy precluded them from annexing the territories so protected. On the other hand, for purposes of annexation the States were treated as foreign territory. It was the accepted policy at the time of Bentinck that these States should be annexed if any suitable opportunity arose. On the plea of misrule, Mysore was put under British administration; and the firm conviction of the Governor-General that the whole of India was bound in course of time to fall under the direct rule of the Company found expression in many other ways. The policy of internal reform to which Bentinck devoted his earnest attention gave him little time to the consideration of questions affecting Indian States, and it was not till the time of Lord Auckland that a definite policy of annexation was laid down as a principle to guide the relationship of the Company with the States.

In 1841, the Court of Directors enunciated the policy "of abandoning no just and honourable accession of territory or revenue." Lord Auckland, Lord Ellenborough, Lord Hastings and Lord Dalhousie were convinced exponents of what has been described as the creed of grab. During their time the Amirates of Sindh, the kingdom of Oudh, the principalities of Satara, Nagpur, Punjab, Jhansi, Tanjore, Jaitpur and numerous other States were annexed to the territories of the Company. Scindia's power was reduced, and he was brought within the system of subsidiary alliance and mulcted of a large portion of his territory. In putting into execution this policy of annextion the authorities of the Company brought to their support the principles of mediæval feudal law and applied rigorously the claims of lapse, escheat, control and confiscation. In 1839, Morvi was declared escheat; Kolaba 'lapsed' in 1840; Surat was annexed in 1842.

It may be remarked *en passant* that during this period the officials of the East India Company were very much under the sway of political theories. The disquisitions of de Tocqueville and de Savigny and others had created a profound interest in feudal idea. Governors-General fresh from England, diplomatists with pretensions of scholarship, and others were easily convinced that the Government of India stood in a feudal relationship with the newly created States. Again, the study of Roman Imperial institutions which Savigny, Momson and others began, and which became popular about the time, provided Anglo-Indian administrators with ideas of imperial supremacy—a scheme in which the Indian States did not appear to fit in. These conditions should be borne in mind while discussing the question of annexation and lapse.

This policy found its culmination in the administration of Lord Dalhousie. In his opinion it was the clear duty of the British Government to confer the blessings of the British rule to the people under the government of Indian Rulers. Wherever therefore he had an opportunity of bringing territories directly under British Rule, he permitted no considerations of treaty or law to stand in his way. As he himself frankly stated 'In States owing to their origin to our grant or gift, if heirs fail according to the terms of our grant, we annex.' So far as that class of States was concerned this principle was rigidly adhered to. But even Dalhousie did not as a general principle accept the idea of sweeping off the board States which did not originate with the British. There were three exceptions to this, and they were Oudh, Nagpur and Satara. The annexation of Oudh was frankly a question of territorial aggrandisement. The Company annexed Oudh on the ground of misgovernment, though Dalhousie himself was against such a procedure as being opposed to inter-national law. But he carried out the policy of the Court of Directors who issued the order on the ground of misgovernment. The whole history of the relationship of Oudh with the Company, from Shuja ud Dowla to Wajid Ali Shah, would show that the responsibility for this misgovernment lay in a great measure with the Company itself.

This is what no less an authority than Sir Henry Lawrence said of Oudh :—

"The facts furnished by every writer on Oudh affairs all testify to the same point, that British interference with that province has been as prejudicial to its Court and people as it has been disgraceful to British name. To quote the words of Col. Sutherland, an able and temperate writer, there is no State in India with whose government we have interfered so systematically and so uselessly as with that of aside." "In short," adds Sir Henry, "wherever we turn we see written in distinct character the blighty influences of our interference."[1] And yet for that misgovernment for which the Company itself was responsible, Oudh was annexed.

Dalhousie himself had on a memorable occasion written as follows :—

"Again, it is often maintained that such is the misgovernment of His Highness the Nizam, that so great are the violence and lawless confusion which pervade every part of his dominions, that it has become the moral duty of the British Government as the paramount power in India to assume to itself the Government of His Highness' dominions in order to correct the evils of his rule and to rescue his subjects from the sufferings which are alleged to proceed therefrom.

"I desire to repudiate all adhesion to a doctrine which leads in my humble judgment to a system of unwarranted and officious meddling.

"In too many instances I fear it proceeds not from sentiments of enlarged benevolence but from the promptings of ambitious greed. Even where the motives from which it springs is pure and sincere, the doctrine is in my view not the less unsound. The acknowledged supremacy of the British power in India gives to it the right, and imposes upon it the duty, of maintaining by its influence and (if need be)

1) Calcutta Review, January, 1845.

compelling by its strength the continuance of general peace. It entitles it to interfere in the administration of Native Princes if their administration tends unquestionably to the injury of the subjects or of the allies of the British Government.

"But I recognise no mission confided to the British Government which imposes on it the obligation or can confer upon it the right of deciding authoritatively on the existence of native independent sovereignties and of arbitrarily setting them aside, whenever their administration may not accord with its own views, and although their acts in no way affect the interests or security of itself or its allies.

"Still less can I recognise any such property in the acknowledged supremacy of the British Government in India as can justify its ruler in disregarding the positive obligations of international contracts, in order to obtrude on Native Princes and their people a system of subversive interference which is unwelcome alike to people and Prince."

No stronger condemnation of the annexation of Oudh is possible than these words written by Dalhousie.

In the case of Nagpur and Satara, Dalhousie's policy was decided, as Lee Warner, his avowed apologist acknowledges, by imperial considerations. These States were placed, says he, right across the main line of communication between Bombay and Madras and Bombay and Calcutta. Consolidation was therefore to be secured by their annexation.

Dalhousie certainly put the coping stone on the edifice, the foundation stone of which had been laid by Clive and which Warren Hastings, Wellesley and the Marquis of Hastings had reared up. The treaty map of India was complete and he had the satisfaction of knowing that the whole of India from Cape Comorin to Kashmir acknowledged the suzerainty of the Queen.

But alas! there was another side to the medal. The India he left was not the India he took over. Under the calm and placid surface of India's waters were gathering all the currents of discontent and hostility occasioned by his high-handed and arbitrary policy towards the States and their Rulers which were soon to converge into a flood which very nearly submerged the British Empire in Hindustan and was powerful enough to wash away in its course the imposing edifice of the East India Company.

LECTURE FOUR

POLITICAL PRACTICE

In this lecture I propose to discuss in some detail the growth of the relationship between Indian States and the Company from the establishment of the Company's paramountcy in 1818 to the time of the assumption of Indian Government by the Crown. So far we have dealt with the policy of the Company's Government towards the States, an aspect of their policy which may properly be called the foreign. With the establishment of paramountcy the relationship became more intimate and, as we have described elsewhere, the Residents became in many States executive officers rather than diplomatic agents. In many of the newly settled tracts like Kathiawad, Bundelkhand and Orissa, the States were maintained as a part of the policy of indirect Government, 'the Government of influence and direction', and naturally a new system of political relationship was brought into being by which the resident political officer practically governed the States through the agency of Indian Rulers. What is now known as Political Practice began to take shape slowly, and it is to this aspect that we should now turn our attention.

Sir John Malcolm who was the most distinguished political officer that Anglo-India produced, and who had taken part in almost every important political settlement from the time of Wellesley, was the statesman responsible for the settlement of Central India. With that rare combination of idealism, practical common sense and realisation of the true tendencies of high policy, he laid down for the benefit of political officers the main principles which he thought ought to guide them in their relations with Indian States. Malcolm laid down the following principles which he considered fundamental. 'If policy requires', says he, 'that we should govern a considerable part of India through the agency of its native princes and chiefs, it is our duty to employ all our moral influence and physical power to strengthen instead of weakening these royal instruments of Government.'[1]

Therefore he argued that the Company must alike avoid 'minute and vexatious interference which counteracts the purpose for which we maintain them by lessening their power and consequently their utility; and that more baneful course which satisfied with their fulfilling the general conditions of their alliance gives a blind support to their authority.'

Secondly, he laid down that as the right of interference in the case of Indian States was limited the political officer should explain the reasons of policy which precludes him from taking such action.[2] This is how he explains this point :

"The Natives of India cannot persuade them-

1) Central India, p. 265.
2) Ibid, p. 446.

selves that, possessing as we do the means of establishing our direct rule, we shall long refrain from doing so. This impression weakens those princes, chiefs and ministers whom it is our policy to support, in a degree that almost unfits them for being instruments of Government. We can only counteract its bad effects by making ourselves understood by all even to the lowest upon this point: it is one on which they will never trust to a communication from any native agent or servant."

Thirdly, that whenever treaties and engagements have to be interpreted "they should be interpreted with much consideration to the prince or chief with whom they are made."[1]

These principles, though laid down primarily in relation to the major rulers, were no less applicable to the minor States. 'In cases of interference with lesser rulers,' says he, 'such as the reformed Rajput plunderers and Bheel Chiefs, we may be compelled to enter more minutely into their affairs; but the principles applied should be the same.'

"Though the check should be efficient," he emphasised that 'it should be unseen—our principle object', he emphasises over and over again, "must be to elevate the authorities to whom we have left the administration of their respective territories: we must in all cases of interference bring them forward to their subjects as the prominent objects of respect and obedience."

1) Central India p. 452.

"It is evident that our control can only be supportable to any human being who has the name and appearance of power so long as it is exercised in a general manner and regulated by the principles above stated. When it descends to minute checks and interference in the collection of revenue, the administration of justice, listens to complaints of discontented or even aggrieved individuals and allows our native agents to interfere and act in the name of the paramount state, the continuance of independent power in any shape to whether prince or chief is not only impolitic but dangerous, as his condition must be felt by himself or by all attached to his person or family as a mockery and degradation; and the least effect of such feelings will be the extermination of all motive to good or great action, for when control is divested of its large and liberal character and takes a more minute shape, whatever merit belongs to the administration becomes the due of the person by whom it is exercised or his agents, and the nominal prince and his officers are degraded into suspected and incompetent instruments of rule."

I have quoted at length from Malcolm because it may truly be said that more than Hastings, more than Wellesley, he was the man who was responsible for the political system of Indian States. Wellesley and the Marquis of Hastings conquered Princes, made treaties and alliances and controlled the destinies of the East India Company. But the political system which was built up on the basis of these alliances was the work of a few men, the most prominent of whom were Malcolm, Metcalfe, Munroe and Elphinstone. It was Malcolm more than anyone else who truly and well elaborated and systematized, as may be seen from the above quotations, the true relationship between the States and the Government.

It should not be understood that these instructions, excellent and unexceptionable as they were, became the accepted lines of conduct all over India. On the other hand, the conditions at the time were so chaotic and unsettled that they remained a dead letter in most places. There was no settled policy yet towards the States. Even with regard to the major States which were at the time said to be in equal alliance, there was neither consistency nor continuity of policy. At one time they would be treated as foreign States in which the Company had no right whatever of interference, as for example in the Bengal political letter of the Marquis of Hastings quoted in the previous lecture; while immediately afterwards a policy of most minute interference in administrative details would be enforced, as again in the case of the Nizam when Chandu Lal, the Prime Minister, was propped up by the authority of the Resident.

This inchoate state of policy is best illustrated in the case of three groups of States which in origin and authority stand apart from the rest of Indian

States. These are the States of Kathiawad, Bundelkhand and the Feudatory States of Bihar and Orissa. The settlement in Kathiawad States we have discussed elsewhere.

We have noticed that by the treaty of 1817 Baji Rao conveyed to the British Government, under Articles 7 and 13, sovereignty of this province in the most specific and absolute form. But his authority over them was only tributary and it was complicated by the fact that the Gaekwar also enjoyed certain suzerain rights. The Gaekwar's rights were also ceded to the Company in 1820.

The position of these States continued to be a matter of doubt and discussion. Their agreements were of a one-sided nature in which they undertook not to harbour robbers and to maintain peace; and they were countersigned as guarantees by other rulers. From the agreements it was by no means clear whether they were merely landholders or tributary States. There was at the same time the consideration that neither the Peishwa nor the Gaekwar could convey to the British Government more than what they themselves possessed; and as the Kathiawad States only acknowledged the suzerainty of the Marathas, the British Government could not claim on the basis of their treaty with the Peishwa and the Gaekwar complete sovereign rights. This was forgotten in 1827, and the Kathiawad States were exempted as a matter of expediency from Bombay Regulation II of 1827. In 1831, with the sanction of the Court of Directors, a Court of Justice presided over by the Political Agent was established; and in fact the Bombay Government continued to contend that the sovereignty over Kathiawad was vested in the British Government and that it was liable to all laws to which the presidency at large was liable.[1] There was great argument, the Governor-General supporting the Bombay view and Sir H. Harrington taking the opposite.

It is only in 1864 that the Secretary of State finally decided that Kathiawad States were not British territory.

The case of Kuch Behar is also interesting.

By the treaty of 1773 the Raja of Kuch Behar agreed "to allow the Kuch Behar country to be annexed to the province of Bengal," and later Kuch Behar was included among the districts of Bengal by section 2 of Regulation III of 1793. The tribute or quit-rent was settled by the Bengal Government and was treated as land revenue, and the question continued to agitate whether it was a State or Estate till it was finally decided that it was not British territory (17th June, 1873).

So far as the Orissa States are concerned, the position is much more interesting. It will be remembered that by the treaty of Deogaon the province of Cuttack was transferred by the Ruler of Nagpur to the Company. Even before the formal session, the Company had negotiated treaties with most of

1) Sir Bartle Frere, Political Despatch, April, 1864.

the tributary Chiefs of Orissa, and Article X of the treaty of Deogaon confirmed them. The allegiance which the Rulers of the Tributary Mahals owed to the Nagpur Government was by this agreement transferred to the British. There was at that time clearly no doubt as to whether these tracts were tributary States, or areas over which Marathas exercised effective sovereignty ; for if they were mere Zamindars, the cession of the province of Cuttack in absolute sovereignty would have included them, and the clause of the treaty of Deogaon itself says that they were feudatories.

In a note by Colonel Ridgeway, a most eminent political officer, the case of the Orissa States is discussed at great length. The engagements with the Chiefs will be found in Volume I of Aitchison's treaties. By these engagements the Chiefs bound themselves "to continue to pay" their "annual Peshkush or tribute," to cause any person "who is an inhabitant of the Sooba appertaining to the Hon'ble Company" who shall flee into their "territory" to be arrested and delivered over ; to extradite any person resident in their State who might commit a crime within Cuttack proper ; to direct their people to sell at fair prices supplies to the "troops of the Hon'ble Company's Government" who "shall pass through my territory" ; and lastly, in certain contingencies "to depute a contingent force of my own troops with the forces of Government."

Though therefore originally there was no doubt as to the semi-independent status of these Rulers, the authorities of Bengal began to act as if this area was territory under the direct sovereignty of the Crown and was in effect British districts. By Regulation IV of 1804, the Criminal Regulations of Bengal were extended to Cuttack, and it was declared that the general regulations in force in Bengal and Bihar shall be in force, unless otherwise specially directed. In this Regulation there was no mention of the Tributary Mahals.

In 1805, Regulations XII, XIII and XIV (regarding revenue administration and criminal and civil justice) were passed. The first of these declared that "nothing herein contained shall be construed to imply that any part of the said regulations are for the present to be considered to be in force in certain jungle or hill Zamindaries occupied by a rude and uncivilized race of people with the proprietors of which estates engagements were formed by the late Board of Commissioners for the payment of a certain quit-rent or tribute to Government". The other Regulations contained an exemption in almost similar language.

In 1804, the Judge and Magistrate of Cuttack had the supervision of the Mahals, but in 1814 he was superseded by a Superintendent Mr. Oswald who was instructed "to establish such a control over the conduct of Zamindars as may prevent the commission of crimes and outrages"; and he was informed that upon the information and suggestions received by him would depend the policy to be pursued with regard to the Mahals. Lord Hastings added :—

"The Governor-General in Council does not understand that such exemption was founded on any claims which the proprietors of these estates have to the exercise of independent authority. On the contrary, His Lordship in Council apprehends that it originated entirely from the opinion which was entertained of the uncivilized manners of the Zamindars themselves and of the inhabitants generally of those places, combined with the nature of the country, which was supposed to consist for the most part of hills and jungles.

"From this short review of the subject, it follows that the continuance of the above-mentioned estates on their present footing is a mere question of expediency and that there is not anything in the nature of our connection with the proprietors of them which should preclude us from placing them under the ordinary jurisdiction of the civil and criminal courts."[1]

It will be noticed that the States had become 'estates' and the Rajas 'proprietors'.

Mr. Impey shortly after succeeded Mr. Oswald and he could have had charge of the office but a few months when, on the 8th July 1814, he submitted to Government a report suggesting that the Regula-

1) Bengal Selections p. 97-98.

tions should be introduced with certain modifications throughout the Mahals. The orders on this report dated 26th July 1814, say that :—

"The Vice-President in Council was not averse to the extension of the General Regulations to the Tributary Mahals, but that before such a measure could be determined much more minute information than had been furnished was necessary."

On the 31st December 1814, the Superintendent again proposed having written laws, and submitted the draft of a Regulation. In the orders dated 21st February 1815, are found these sentiments :—"The Vice-President in Council considered it probable that the ignorance and prejudices of the proprietors of some of the Tributary Mahals might induce them to oppose the introduction of the Regulations and to resist all such orders of the Court as they might conceive to be discreditable to their personal rank or calculated to weaken their influence and authority in their respective estates, and it could not be expected that such resistance would in every instance be subdued without the employment of a military force. The adoption of coercive measures in the Tributary Mahals would not under any circumstances be resorted to by Government without great reluctance. The Vice-President in Council would be disposed to introduce the Criminal Regulations without further delay, if he were assured that they could be duly carried into execution without the necessity of employing any military force for that purpose."

In 1815 again the propriety of extending the Regulations was canvassed and a draft was actually approved by the Court of Nizamat Adalat ; but in submitting the papers to Government, it appears the third Judge of the Court, Mr. Stewart, forwarded a minute expressing his doubts whether the country was prepared for such a change. He further raised the point as to how far States like Mayurbhanj which exercised "an independent authority under the protection of the British Government," were liable to be subjected to ordinary municipal jurisdiction. Finally, Regulation XI of 1816 containing rules for the conduct of suits respecting claims to the right of succession in these Mahals, was passed, but the introduction of criminal laws was abandoned.

On the 21st June 1816, the Secretary to Government tells the Superintendent :—

"The office of Superintendent was constituted expressly to supply in a certain degree the want of more regular establishments. It is not the object of Government to weaken the influence of the Rajas of the Tributary Mahals over their peasantry and still less to interfere in the details of usages of the country. It is sufficient that you should adopt such prudent and proper measures as may tend to prevent the commission of acts of violence and outrage by the interposition of your influence, and by encouraging amicable adjustment of disputes when circumstances will admit of an interference of that nature. Were the duties of your office really incapable of being conducted on the principles above stated, it would follow that the office itself was useless and might consequently be abolished. In that case the only remaining alternative would be either to extend the Regulations to the Tributary Mahals or to leave the proprietors to their own guidance and to the exercise of the same authority which they exercised previously to the appointment of a Superintendent for their control."

During 1817-20, the Tributary Mahals attracted little notice. In 1821, the Raja of Keonjhur having behaved ill by obstructing the passage of some troops through his country, and the Raja of Nyaghar having afforded an asylum to and protected a rebel, on the 11th July and 7th September 1821, the Superintendent Mr. Blunt in his reports bearing those dates represented that he was not aware in what manner an offender could be legally proceeded against and brought to punishment; that he disapproved of the rules which had been in 1815 proposed by Mr. Impey and he submitted rules which he proposed to introduce to prevent the perpetration of crimes of magnitude with impunity, and to provide for the speedy regular trial of persons accused of such offences. These letters were considered by the Government on the 17th December 1821, and a resolution was recorded, paragraph 51 of which says:—"His Excellency in

Council wholly concurs with the Commissioner in the opinion as to the expediency of providing formally for the administration of criminal justice in the Tributary Estates exempt from the operation of the Regulations. The draft rules submitted by the Commissioner are generally approved, and will be enacted into a Regulation with such modifications as are judged necessary, under the title of a Regulation for the administration of criminal justice in certain Hill Estates of Cuttack exempt from the operations of the general laws." But this project of legislation was never carried into effect.

In 1839 the Superintendent, Mr. Ricketts, suggested the introduction of a regular system of management, and he submitted a draft of Civil and Criminal rules in which he also defined the authority which the Rajas as Criminal and Civil Judges might exercise within their own territories. These rules were disapproved as being in their general scope of too extensive a nature, and involving more interference than was desirable[1] and as tending to weaken injuriously the influence of the Rajas over their subjects : and Mr. Mills was directed to revise them on the principles explained in the letter from the officiating Secretary to the Government of India in the Legislative Department, dated 25th November 1839, No. 470, which interdicted the Rajas from inflicting the punishment of death or any other

1) Bengal Selections p. 59-61.

punishment contrary to the principles of English law, from committing enormities upon the people of their countries or harrassing or attacking their neighbours and enjoined as little interference as possible in matters either of civil or criminal justice. Mr. Mills adopted Mr. Ricketts' rules as his groundwork, modifying only such parts as involved too great an interference in the general administration of civil and criminal justice, and adding some suggestions of his own, the principal of which provided for the abolition of Merriah sacrifices and Suttee; but the Government of India considering them to be by far too minute and precise to work well, directed him to "draw out some short, clear and well-defined rules, making the Rajas responsible to the Superintendent in cases of murder, homicide and other henious offences without, however, interfering so far as to make them amenable to the civil court of the Superintendent in cases between the Rajas and their creditors."

Rules revised on the above principles were accordingly submitted: the Government of India thought it better not to pass any regular and defined rules at least for the present, but directed the Superintendent to shape his conduct by the spirit of those proposed. "Guided by these rules," wrote Mr. Mills, "it has been my constant aim to abstain as much as possible from all gratuitous and unnecessary interference with the Chiefs in their affairs except where I could interpose my authority to encourage or promote an amicable adjustment of disputes."

In 1841, the Court of Directors ordered the abolition of Suttee. This prohibition was notified to the Chiefs, and in 1842 they were required to enter into an engagement to prevent Suttee. In this they wrote, "We engage unhesitatingly to submit ourselves to any penal orders which the Superintendent of the Tributary Mahals may issue if we shall act in any way contrary to the engagements of this recognizance."

In 1845, Act XXI was passed for suppression of Merriah sacrifices in the Hill Tracts of Orissa and other places. This gave the Governor-General in Council power to remove from the jurisdiction of the Superintendent any of the Tributary Mahals and to place them under the jurisdiction and superintendence of an officer designated the Agent for the Suppression of Merriah sacrifices, who was to be guided by rules prescribed by the Governor-General in Council. These rules, mong other things, were to define the jurisdiction of the Sadar Court. This Act (now repealed) appears never to have been enforced in the Mahals.

In 1840, the Tributary State of Banki was annexed, owing to the Raja having been convicted of murder—a summary proceeding which was natural in Lord Auckland's time but which will not be imitated now. In 1847, Angul, another Tributary State, was confiscated owing to the Raja's attempt to wage war against Government. Both States have since been treated as British territory and have been scheduled under Act XIV of 1874.

In 1850, Act XX was enacted for settling disputed boundaries between the Tributary Mahals "and estates subject to the Regulations of the Bengal Code."

In 1851, the Bengal Government appointed the Magistrate of Midnapur to be ex-officio Assistant Superintendent to enable him to communicate direct with the Tributary Chiefs on the occurrence of crime.

This kind of action continued; the Bengal Government for the most part treating the States as part of British territory, and the Government of India trying hard to resist the temptation. The matter was not finally settled and the area formally declared foreign territory, till the decision of the Calcutta High Court in Keshab Mahajan's case.[1] This was followed by Act XI of 1893, repealing all references to the Orissa States in the Regulations.

It would be clear from the facts stated above in what state of inconsistency and chaotic contradiction the policy towards Indian States was in the period between the Marquis of Hastings, when the Company began to assert the claims of paramountcy, and the Mutiny when the Crown assumed the right of suzerainty. The authorities of the Company were wavering with every passing fancy as to whether the Rulers were Zamindars, feudatories, tributaries or

1) Indian Law Reports, Calcutta Series, Volume VIII. (1882) p. 985.

independent sovereigns; and each Governor-General and each Resident held and enforced his own views. These words were so loosely used that in relation to Afghanistan and Nepal, two States admittedly out of the Indian political system, the political officers often used words which are now considered objectionable in the case of minor Indian States. Sir Lepil Griffin writing about Amir Abdur Rahman remarks as follows :—

"To-day the Ruler of Afghanistan conducts his administration on principles similar to those of Ranjit Singh, yet the British Government with whom *he is in subordinate and feudatory alliance* does not offer a remonstrance." The Maharajas whose territorial sovereignty was not denied were alluded to as Zamindars or proprietors, and States like Indore and Baroda which were in alliance with the Company were spoken of as feudatories. Kutch Behar was called an Estate. This extraordinary variety and looseness of terminology tended to obscure the true relationship between the Company and the States and to confuse the issues. A rough and ready line was followed of interfering in States where interference was safe and letting alone those who by their strength or by their position were able to withstand such encroachment. The States that suffered most from this policy of unchecked interference were those whose connection with the Company was the longest: Oudh, Travancore, Hyderabad and Baroda. In Oudh, the Nawab Wazir was permitted to assume the Kingly title, but nothing remained of the powers which Shah Shuja had once exercised. The evils which Malcolm had foreseen of the corroding influence of minute interference which would tend to reduce the rulers to a degrading mockery of royalty, had actually occured in Oudh where the Ruler had become a puppet.

King Nasiruddin Shah was made to sign a treaty in 1834, by which he agreed to sign any new treaty which the Governor-General may dictate. In Hyderabad, the long reign of Secunder Jah was a standing testimony to the paralysing effects of interference. The species of interference that weakens and unsettles had full play in the Nizam's court,where the Prime Ministers took orders from the Residents and were in alliance with the financial firm of Palmer and Co., to whom a large portion of the State was mortgaged. The disorganization consequent upon this system of irresponsibility was so great that at one time it was proposed to appoint British Commissioners for the provinces. In Travancore, the Resident Colonel Munro took over the administration and combined the functions of Dewan and Resident.

As we have mentioned before, even this policy of interference was not consistently followed. The Government of the Company watched with indifference misrule in many States. The explanation for this is provided by the fact that from the time of the Marquis of Hastings up to the Mutiny all the

Governors-General were convinced that the assumption of direct Government by the Company over these areas was the only solution. In Bundelkhand, Kathiawad and Orissa they frankly declared that the Rulers were only Zamindars holding from the Company. In the case of better established States with treaties of alliances, the Company could either intervene, or, when misgovernment became bad enough, annex.

The vagueness and the lack of consistency of this policy, which at one moment would interfere in minute affairs of administration and at another leave the ruler free to do anything he chose, came to a close only with the Mutiny. It is not our purpose to discuss in these lectures the causes and events that led to that catastrophe; but it may summarily be stated that it was an epitaph written in blood of the chaotic, indefinite and contradictory policy pursued towards the States.

LECTURE FIVE

SOVEREIGNTY AND INTER-STATAL LAW

As a logical corollary of the conception of the States in alliance being independent and foreign, principles of International Law were considered to be binding in the relations between the Company's Government and the States. Thus in the case of Coorg, war was actually declared against the Raja who was accused of conducting himself against the principles of international law. So late as 1855, when the proposal for the annexation of Oudh was being strongly pressed on him, Dalhousie wrote: "The course proposed by the Court is not warranted by international law. It would be either conquest or usurpation of the power of Government by force of arms."[1] His despatch already quoted in connection with intervention in Hyderabad, also proves it.

Yet at the same time, side by side with this vague idea of the principles of international law, there was developing a system of public law consequent on the claims of suzerainty and the assumption of the outward forms of sovereignty by the Company. The Company originally held their lands by grant from Indian Powers and therefore claimed no rights of sovereignty. Only when the Company conquered territories, the

1) Dalhousie's letters, p. 363.

sovereignty came to the British Crown. In the Dewani districts, and in other areas acquired under the nominal sovereignty of Indian Princes like the Northern Circars, the Company administered as Rulers, but in theory they were only agents or lease-holders. Externally, in relation to the French and others they claimed a special position, but from the point of view of internal sovereignty the Company was content to take shelter under the wide wings of the Moghul or of his Subedars. The sovereignty of the Company over the areas under occupation was exercised but not avowed. But the external position continued to be anomalous, for in the treaties with Foreign Powers, British sovereignty in India is clearly stated.

In relation to the Moghul, the Company was originally in the position of an ordinary Dewan entrusted with revenue administration of Bengal, Bihar and Orissa. The Viceroy of the province was the Nawab Nazim of Murshidabad. When the Company finally assumed his powers and relegated him to the position of a nominal ruler, they did not interfere with the claims of the Moghul Emperor. Hastings, however, refused the payment of the tribute to the Emperor, but Mahdaji Scindia as Deputy Administrator-General of the Empire continued to put forward the claim as long as he lived.

Cornwallis was the first Governor-General who took up the question of the Company's theoretical dependence on the Moghul. He omitted in his correspondence with the Emperor the terms denoting vassalage and obedience. At the time of Nasir-ul-Mulk's succession to the Suba of Bengal, Cornwallis recognised him without the Nawab having received a sanad from the Emperor, in spite of the protest of Mahdàji as Vakil-i-Mutlak on behalf of Shah Alum. In 1803 when Lord Lake entered Delhi, Shah Alum received him and invested him with a khillat and a title. Though Shah Alum became a prisoner of the Company, the fiction of their ruling in his name was too convenient to be discarded, and the authorities of the Company continued to show him all the outward forms of obedience.

The position underwent a radical change in the time of the Marquis of Hastings. The Moghul Emperor had asked that the Governor-General should visit him. This is how the Governor-General himself states the position :—

"Mr. Metcalfe arrived from Delhi. The King had been carrying on a wearisome negotiation with him to obtain that I should visit him. Mr. Metcalfe always returned the same answer—namely that I had expressed myself very desirous of paying my personal attentions to His Majesty, but had told him (Metcalfe) that I was restrained from doing so by the knowledge that His Majesty expected my acquiescence in a ceremonial which was to imply His Majesty's being the Liege lord of British possessions. This dependent tenure Mr. Metcalfe assured him could never be acknowledged by him...... Nothing has kept up the floating notion of a duty owed to the Imperial family but our gratuitous and persevering exhibition of their pretensions—an exhibition attended with much servile obeisance in the etiquette imposed upon us by the ceremonial of the court."

As the Emperor refused to yield the point, the interview did not take place. Lord Hastings, however, had other methods of reducing the Royal pretensions of the Moghul. He encouraged the Wazir of Oudh to assume the Royal title in order that the Emperor may no longer be under the delusion that the princes and powers of India were under his nominal sway.

In the time of Lord Amherst, Akbar II who occupied the throne of Delhi agreed to receive the Governor-General without the usual formalities. The reason why Akbar II yielded on the question was explained by him to the Resident as follows :—

"He had been influenced by an apprehension of the consequences similar to those which had resulted from the objection which His Majesty had urged to a meeting with the Marquis of Hastings on the footing then proposed, as he expressly stated this caused the subsequent assumption by the Nawab Wazir of the title of King ; that in the hope of obviating these consequences he had reluctantly acquiesced in the ceremonial established by Lord Amherst."[1]

1) Punjab Government Records, Delhi Residency, Vol. I. p. 367.

The ceremonial form of address was altered. It was in order to represent these matters to the British Government that Rāja Rammohan Roy was sent as the Moghul Ambassador to England. The letter from the Moghul Emperor to the King of England which was entrusted to Rammohan Roy read as follows :—"All the Governors-General who have preceded Lord Amherst in the Government of the British territories in India have thought it no degradation to themselves to address me or my august father in the style that custom has accorded to Royalty. Lord Amherst, however, thought proper to reduce me in form of communication to the footing of an equal......so as to humble me in the eyes of all ranks of people." But his embassy was not recognised and nothing came of it. Coins were still struck in the Emperor's name. Only in 1835, the right of independent coinage bearing the image of the British Sovereign was assumed; and the system of paying Nazar to the phantom Emperor was stopped only in the time of Ellenborough.

With the assertion of sovereign claims, the attitude of suzerainty over the minor States also developed. The Company stood forth as a suzerain who had the authority as well as the power to depose rulers and interfere in all details of internal administration. This we have already noticed in relation to the growth of the power of the Residents. But the position was peculiar as an eminent English writer has put it :—

"Yet all this vast fabric of supremacy rests upon the foundation of a Royal Grant which is subject to be revoked at any time if the advisers of the British Crown are dissatisfied with the conduct of the Company and is exercised from day to day at the discretion of a royal officer.... And behind all stands the reserved supremacy of the Imperial Parliament which could by legislation make any alteration it pleased with the constitution and position of the Company or even abolish it altogether. Clearly then it is no independent authority in the eyes of British law but a subordinate body controlled by the appropriate departments of the Supreme Government. Like Janus of old it has two faces. On that which looks towards the native population all the lineaments and attributes of sovereignty are majestically outlined; on that which is turned towards the United Kingdom is written subordination and submission."[1]

The public law that developed as a result of this assumption of suzerain authority dealt with five questions. They are: (1) The independence of States; (2) Property; (3) Jurisdiction; (4) Ceremonials and (5) Diplomacy. Each of these requires careful enquiry and study, but for the purpose of these lectures they are only summarily treated here.

So far as the question of independence is concerned, it is clear that all the States in subordinate alliance surrendered their external relations to the

1) Lawrence: Principles of International Law.

Company. Thus they ceased to be independent powers from the point of view of international law. But their internal independence was guaranteed, some in the most absolute manner and others in more limited phraseology. But even here a policy of intervention developed as we have noticed, by which the Company assumed rights to regulate succession, to refuse or recognise adoption, to suggest methods for better government and in general to advise the Rulers. As a consequence of this loss of external independence, the States also lost the right of making peace and war among themselves. The Company, on the other hand, had the obligation of defending the States from internal and external enemies and of safe-guarding their interests in other countries. Thus when Travancore was attacked by Tipu, the Company had to lead an expedition against the Ruler of Mysore. When the States on the border of the Punjab feared the attacks of Ranjit Singh, the Company had to intervene. The Company undertook the obligation of maintaining the Princes against internal rebellion also.

The main question on which the internal sovereignty of the States was disregarded on the basis of a theory of suzerainty, was in relation to succession. Sir John Shore had interfered to set aside a succession in Oudh. When Secunder Jah succeeded to the Masnad of Hyderabad, he had sought the recognition of the Moghul and the Company. In the States closely allied to the

Company, the political authorities regulated succession as a matter of practice. But in the States which were recognised to be in independent alliance, a different policy was followed. Thus when Maharaja Dowlat Rao Scindia was lying ill in 1828, the Government of India urged him to adopt a successor, adding however "that the British Government did not pretend to any right to control or regulate succession to the State of Gwalior as the Maharaja as the absolute Ruler of the country should be considered to possess the undoubted right of determining the succession." The same view was held in the Bahawalpur case. But in the State of Indore, when Maharaja Khande Rao Holkar died in February 1844, the Government of India thinking that the accession of Martand Rao, the legitimate heir, would have the appearance of a succession by a legitimate right, was desirous of finding another candidate so that "the selection of a successor should be manifestly the sole act of the British Government as the protecting Paramount State."[1] This principle was generally followed with regard to all the States during the time of Ellenborough, Hardinge and Dalhousie.

So far as property rights are concerned, the States continued to possess their independence except in the following cases :—

1. When such property rights brought a State into conflict with other States, as in boundary

1) Despatch No. 88, p. 82.

disputes, the Suzerain Power claimed final authority for decision. The leading example of this kind of right is in the claims and counter-claims between Travancore and Cochin, and between the States of Kathiawad. A more definite case of the limitation of the right of property in the relation between Indian States and the Government of India, is in the guarantee given by the Paramount Power to the Jagirdars and feudatories of the States. This is a vast and very important subject into which I have not the time to enter today. But a few examples may be quoted here for reference. The mediatised estates of Gwalior, the Bhomias of Udaipur and the Jaredas of Cutch are Jagirdars and noblemen who held guarantees from the British Government which effectively restricted the authority of their sovereign over them. There are numerous cases in which the guarantee operated to set up these estates as separate States independent of the State under which they held the Jagir. The case of Jaora in regard to Indore, of Kichilpur and Ratlam in regard to Gwalior, and of the Kathiawad States in relation to the Gaekwar, explain this tendency. These States were subordinate feudatories of the Rulers mentioned above, but in course of time as a result of the restriction of authority implied in the guarantee, they became separate States enjoying various degrees of independence.

2. There are cases where the Company thought it necessary to establish a monopoly. The cases which

are of importance in this connection as limiting the definite rights of property of the States, deal with the production of salt and opium. As early as 1829, the Government of Bombay began to interfere in the production of salt of the Radhanpur State. In 1829, the salt works of the State were made joint property of the Durbar and the British Government. In 1837, the Government suggested that the whole of the salt works of Radhanpur should be surrendered for a money compensation. This policy, however, was systematically followed only in the post-Mutiny period when the Government of India set itself to acquire a monopoly of salt by agreement with other States.

In regard to opium, the case is similar. Warren Hastings revived the Moghul monopoly of opium in Bengal, Behar and Orissa. The system of monopoly was extended to the territories that came under the Company. The trade in Malwa opium was seen to interfere in the China trade of the Company; and in 1803, a measure was passed prohibiting the export of Malwa opium from Bombay ports. As the export of opium continued in spite of this prohibition, agreements were proposed with Baroda, Indore and other States "limiting cultivations, prohibiting the sale of drugs and its transit through the States and requiring it to be made over at a fixed price to the British agent at Indore who was to buy up the whole crop and to send it to Bombay for sale at a profit." This policy met with no success and had to be given up. The territories of Gujrat, Kathiawad and Cutch still came under the prohibition. The policy of prohibition was, however, universally enforced at a later time.

Various restrictions on property rights exist in the Orissa States.

In the matter of jurisdiction, it is important to note that in the days before the Mutiny the main States enjoyed complete jurisdiction over all persons within its territory including Europeans. The restrictions with regard to Europeans was introduced in the period between 1862-1869. But during the period under consideration the territorial nature of jurisdiction was fully admitted by the Government of India, and Indian States exercised freely their right of jurisdiction over Europeans of all nationalities. It may also be noticed here that in many treaties—for example, in the treaty with Bhopal—there are express provisions that British law and jurisdiction will not be introduced within that principality. In Kathiawad, however, the position was different. The Rulers themselves had to execute a security bond that they will not have feud with any other Talukdars, that they will not harbour outlaws, that they will not incite any person to commit any act of violence, that they will not harbour thieves or plunder others on the high road or commit robbery. As a result of the constant quarrels between these States and also of the doubt that existed at the time as to the status of these States, a Court of Justice presided over by the Agent was established which effectively restricted their rights of jurisdiction. In Orissa and Nagpur States also the jurisdictional power of the rulers was greatly restricted.

The jurisdictional independence of the States also suffered through the establishment of cantonments within the States. In Secunderabad within the Nizam's territory, where the British troops are stationed, the law administered was always British law. But in Gwalior, in 1853 the Government of India recognised that the sovereignty of Gwalior extended intact over the cantonment areas and that the Government of India had no sovereign right either to set up criminal courts or try persons committing offences within those areas or to legislate for them. His Highness, however, granted a sanad authorising the establishment of such courts. This was maintained with regard to Gwalior. But the Gwalior case was exceptional; and generally the principle followed was where the British were in effective occupation, jurisdiction vested in the Company.

The other main question with regard to jurisdiction relates to extradition. Extradition has been defined as the surrender by one State to another of an individual who is found within the territory of the former and is accused of having committed a crime within the territory of the latter. Ramses II of Egypt made a treaty of this nature with Khutsir, king of Khita.

There are numerous agreements mainly with minor States which provide for the surrender of criminals. With some States there are extradition treaties. In 1836, however, the Court of Directors held that British subjects apprehended in British territory for offences committed within Indian States should in no case be surrendered. Curiously enough it was also held by them that subjects of Indian States even when apprehended outside British India should be amenable to British courts for offences committed within British territory. It need hardly be said that this is not the practice now.

In the matter of ceremonials there was, during the period which we are discussing, as there is to-day, much trouble. A visit from Dalhousie to Jammu could not take place, as no agreement could be reached between Gulab Singh and the Viceroy on the question of ceremonials. It should, however, be remembered that the present position with regard to the salutes, precedence, rank etc. dates only from 1877. Before the Mutiny the Company was not meticulous about these matters. They did not care very much to regulate ceremonials except when they affected the status of the Company's own officers.

In matters of diplomacy, the Resident, though he started as a Minister established on a reciprocal basis, soon became the sole channel of communication. Vakils from Indian Courts continued to reside at the Viceregal Court for a considerable time; but after the break up of the Maratha confederacy their position became formal. From the earliest times the Resident's person was considered inviolable and any attack on him was considered an act of war. The alleged attempt on the Resident at Poona was one of the causes of the war against Baji Rao the last Peishwa. The case against Apa Sahib of Nagpur was also the same. The Resident also enjoyed its ex-territoriality for the area in which he resided. He himself and his staff were exempt from customs and other dues. The formalities regarding his official interviews were strictly regulated.

This body of semi-international law which slowly grew up between the time of the Marquis of Hastings and the Mutiny was, it needs hardly be said, still inchoate. In fact, it is well known that until recently there was no attempt to codify or to lay down authoritatively the practice in most of these matters which continued to be applied as circumstances dictated in each particular case. But what is of importance is that the period under consideration witnessed the growth of a general body of practice in these matters, and these laid the foundation of what is compendiously known as Indian political practice.

LECTURE SIX

FINANCIAL RELATIONS

In 1818, practically the whole of India outside the Punjab passed under British authority. Sometime before this the Company also ceased to be a trading corporation. With the complete divorce of commercial activities, the Company became more and more interested in the development of India as a market for British goods and as a producer of raw material for British manufacture. The era of peace which followed the Napoleonic wars, was the era of industrial expansion and commercial development. The revolution in transport consequent upon the use of steam power for Railways and ships, led to such an expansion in trade as would have staggered the imagination of the early commercial adventurers who opened up the trade of India.

The great difficulty that stood in the way of the organization of India as a great market for English goods, was the interspersing of British territories with the Indian States. At every turn outside Bengal, Indian States broke up the continuous line of communication. Between Bombay, the great sea-port, and Delhi, the great emporium of North Indian trade, lay the territories of Gwalior, Bhopal and numerous petty States. In fact, even in 1818 the main portion of the hinterland of India was occupied by these independent principalities.

There were two alternatives open to the Government of India if it wanted to unite their scattered territories. Either the States could be treated as inconvenient blocks of foreign territory which stood in the way of the development of the commercial and economic potentialities of British Provinces, or as being allies with whom a common policy of economic co-operation could be worked out. The first involved the idea of annexation whenever suitable opportunities arose in order that these obstacles may be removed. The second involved economic penetration and political subordination which the Princes at that time would not have accepted. Besides, the official view was that these States were foreign territories in the strict sense of the term.

Thus from the time the Company began to interest itself in economic development, the question of acquiring territory took a new turn. This policy is best explained in the following narrative of Hope in his book on the House of Scindia.

"A demi-official letter was written to the Resident by the Chief Secretary of the Foreign Department desiring him to learn at a private interview by way of a feeler, if the Maharaja encircled as he was by serious troubles, mainly caused by our Government, would like to resign, assigning over the country to the British Government and receiving a handsome pension, which would be paid out by his own revenues. Mr. Cavendish than whom no Englishman attained a greater ascendency over the minds of the Natives with whom he had concern declined to make such a suggestion, and his answer threw a damp upon the hope of the annexationists. The Government officials were of course extremely angry. Presently another demi-official letter arrived, this time from the Deputy Secretary of the Foreign Department, strongly expostulating with Mr. Cavendish for his proceedings and ending with the significant remark, "*You have thus allowed a favourable chance to escape of connecting Agra to the Bombay Presidency.*"

The question of opening up the Indus as a channel of navigation was also taken up at this time. For the purpose of surveying the Indus it was proposed to send a deputation with presents to Ranjit Singh *via* Scinde. Metcalfe who was a member of the Council at that time protested against this. In a strongly worded minute he stated as follows :—

"The scheme of surveying the Indus under the pretext of sending a present to Raja Ranjeet Singh seems to be highly objectionable. It is a trick in my opinion unworthy of our Government, which cannot fail, when detected, as most probably it will be, to excite the jealousy and indignation of the powers on whom we play it. It is just such a trick as we are often falsely suspected and accused of by the native powers of India, and this confirmation of their suspicions, generally unjust, will do us more injury by furnishing the ground of merited reproach than any advantage to be gained by the measure can compensate."

This point of view of acquiring Indian sovereignties which lay interspersed with British territories, thus obstructing the lines of communication, was at the bottom of the annexationist policy followed from 1830 to 1857. In fact, Lord Dalhousie declared :—

"I take occasion of recording my strong and deliberate opinion that in the exercise of a wise and sound policy the British Government is bound not to put aside or neglect such rightful opportunities of acquiring territory or revenue as may from time to time present themselves."[1] In his negotiations with Hyderabad regarding the lease of territory in exchange of annual payments for the maintenance of subsidiary forces, Dalhousie pitched upon Berar on this principle. The motive is frankly explained by the Governor-General himself, in his Despatch dated 28th February, 1856 :—

"In the possession of Berar and the neighbouring districts the British Government, it deserves to be remembered, has secured the finest cotton tracts which are known to exist in all the continent of India and thus has opened up a great additional channel of supply through which to make good a felt deficiency in the staple of one great branch of its manufacturing industry."

Trade relations with Indian States also gave rise

1) Arnold, Administration of the Marquis of Wellesley, II, p. 119.

to a definite policy. The transit duties in Indian States, through which British goods had to pass, were a source of trouble.

As early as 1798, the Company had secured from Hyderabad the abolition of Rahdarry duties and the fixation of State customs at 5 per cent. Other interferences with trade we have alluded to in our previous lecture.

The financial relation with the States may also be touched upon here. In the early days adventurers in the service of the Company found it profitable to lend sums to Indian Rulers who were in close alliance with the Company. The chief Ruler who became the victim of his debts was Nawab Mohammad Ali of Arcot. He was advanced money at usurious interests by these men, and in exchange he assigned the revenues of certain districts to them. There is a very large literature on the Nawab of Arcot's debts and the dealings of a very mysterious person called Mr. Paul Benfield. Some of the Nawab's creditors were members of the Madras Council. The Nawab's whole State was at one time assigned to the Company, but at the clamorous protest of his creditors it was given back. The Nawab started again in his career of financial extravagance and borrowed much larger sums at least on paper. In 1787, a partition of the revenues of the State was made by which nine lakhs of pagodas were reserved for the State and twelve for the creditors. Finally Carnatic was annexed. But the transactions *with* regard to Carnatic debt had one beneficent result, and that was the Parliamentary prohibition of loan by Europeans to Indian Rulers. This was a very necessary safeguard then, however obsolete we may consider its provisions now. It saved the major States from following the disastrous path which Mohammad Ali trod, and which Khédive Ismail of Egypt was at a later time to follow with equally painful results.

The story of the Carnatic was not repeated in India; but the transactions of Messrs. Palmer & Co., in Hyderabad demonstrated what difficulties Indian States might be put to if the activities of financial adventurers were not regulated and watched. Palmer & Co., which was a firm of bankers, entered into financial transactions with the Nizam's Minister Chandu Lal who followed the easy policy of covering up holes by darkness. The British subsidy had to be paid; the State had to be administered; if it was impossible to raise revenue by which to do these things, it could easily be arranged by loans. Palmer & Co., were willing to advance whatever the Nizam's government wanted. This system crippled the Hyderabad State, and it was saved only by the decisive interference of Sir Charles Metcalfe.

Though in the Carnatic and Hyderabad the financial transactions were thus of a kind which profited private European adventurers and firms, the general position with regard to other States improved greatly owing to the experience of Mohammad

Ali and Secunder Jah. Private financiers could not lend money to States. The ruin of Palmer & Co., had made exploitation by firms equally difficult. The Rulers had no armies to keep, and no proper administrations to maintain. The present policy of progressive expenditure in roads, education, etc., was hardly thought of. The result was that the Princes accumulated money. The Company was not slow to take advantage of this circumstance and generally turned to the Rulers of States in case of financial difficulty. Thus in 1814, Ghias-ud-Din Hyder, the Nawab Vizier of Oudh, lent the Company the 2½ million pounds with which the Nepal expedition was financed. In 1825, Oudh, which had earned the sobriquet of having been the wetnurse of the Company, lent another million pounds. In 1826, again half a million was advanced by the accommodating Ruler of Oudh. Baiza Baye of Gwalior lent £8,00,000, while smaller States like Nagpur lent in proportion. Even the unfortunate Baji Rao lent money to the Company out of the savings of his pension. Ellenborough borrowed another £1,00,000 from Oudh in the days when Oudh was supposed to be groaning under mis-government.

While the Rulers amassed money, as is evident from the above transactions, the administration of the States degenerated with great rapidity. There is not one among the Rulers of India in the period between 1818 and 1857 who stands out as a statesman or even as a moderately able Prince.

Nor was it their fault. In all the States where the Company was accustomed to intervene in internal affairs, they had systematically followed the policy of nominating the Dewans and maintaining them in authority. In Baroda, it was only long after the Mutiny that the rule was abolished requiring the Gaekwar to obtain the sanction of Government for the appointment of his Dewan. In Travancore and Cochin, the principle was officially laid down that the Rajas could not remove their Dewans without the sanction of the Madras Government. From the time of the Travancore rebellion in 1809, to the time of Sir T. Madhava Rao, the Dewans of that State were generally some low paid officials of the Residency. The same was the case in Hyderabad where the Ministers were appointed at the suggestion of the Residency, and in Oudh where the Resident had the final voice in the selection. The effects of this system were thus described by Sir Henry Lawrence in an article in the *Calcutta Review* of January, 1848 :—

"If ever there was a device for insuring mal-government, it is that of a native Ruler and Minister both relying on foreign bayonets and directed by a British Resident. Even when all three are able, virtuous and considerate, still the wheels of government could hardly move smoothly. Each of the three may work incalculable mischief but no one of them can do good if thwarted by the others."

The evil results of this system were noticed from the very beginning of the days when protected

States came into existence. "From the reports I have received from Residents," Cornwallis wrote to Lord Lake, "I am sorry to find that the States who are intimately connected with us are reduced to the most forlorn condition; that these powers possess no funds or troops on which they can depend, that anarchy and disaffection prevail universally throughout their dominions." Sir Thomas Munro observed the same results. "Wherever the subsidiary system is introduced," he wrote, "the country will soon bear the marks of it, in decaying villages and decreasing population." This has long been observed in the dominions of the Nizam and the Peishwa.

The history of Indian States during the period between the Marquis of Hastings and the Mutiny is a sad, if illuminating, commentary on this text. Oudh which was the nearest State to the Company's capital was in a state of perpetual mal-administration. In 1839, Dr. Butler who had opportunities of seeing for himself the conditions in Oudh wrote as follows :—

"The administrative state of the country may be summed up in a few words. A sovereign regardless of the interests of his kingdom except so far as it supplies him with the means of personal indulgence, a minister incapable or unwilling to stay the ruin of the country, local governors, or more properly speaking farmers of revenue, invested with virtually despotic powers left almost unchecked to gratify their rapacity and private enmities, a local army ill paid and therefore licentious and habituated to defeat, an almost absolute denial of justice in all matters civil and criminal, and an overwhelming British force distributed through the province."

Revenue was collected by force. Plunderers infested the country. Colonel Sleeman states that frightful tortures were common. In Lucknow there was a Saddar Court. But the people in authority were the King's eunuchs and other menials. It is said that the King appointed his favourite fiddler to be the Chief Justice. Nor were the members of the royal family treated better. General Outram received a petition from 216 ladies of the Palace representing that they had not received their stipends for many years. This intolerable condition was, as we have seen, inevitable when authority was so divided and the sovereign had no sense of responsibility and well knew that his position did not depend upon the contentment of his subjects but on the friendship of the Company. To the Company the Rulers of Oudh were religiously loyal, a fact that every writer acknowledges.

The position in Hyderabad was no better. The long reign of Secunder Jah witnessed the thorough ruin of the financial system of the Nizam's Government and proposals were made more than once for putting the State temporarily under British administration. The treasury was bankrupt, the administration hopelessly corrupt, violence and lawless confusion pervaded every part of the dominions.

It was only the administrative and diplomatic genius of Salar Jung that saved Hyderabad from annexation. The position in Mysore was no better. After Purniah's fall the administration of the State followed the same monotonous course as in Oudh and Hyderabad. A committee was appointed to enquire into Mysore affairs and on its report the administration was taken over temporarily by the Government. Affairs in Indore were no better. The administration of Maharajah Hari Rao was so unbearable that his own people beseiged him in his palace and tried to assassinate him. In Baroda, Ananda Rao Gaekwar's administration led to financial ruin. His creditors could not be paid. It was proposed to annex Cochin on the ground of maladministration. In Rajputana States there was a perpetual fight between the Thakurs of the Rulers, and in this fight the State administration counted for nothing. In Gwalior, the guaranteed nobles, the Maratha Jagirdars and the Ruler each contributed his share to the anarchy.

This break down of the government of Indian States was due to the transitional character of the period. The Rulers ceased to have any fear of losing their State by external attack or by internal rebellion. The modern idea of administration had not developed. The subsidiary system and the system of administration though nominated Dewans had resulted in this catastrophe.

The alternatives before the British Government

were either to annex these States or evolve a policy which would reconcile the conflicting ideas of the independence of the Rulers and the responsibility of the British Government for better Government. In the period before the Mutiny the authorities of the Company thought that the only solution lay in annexation whenever suitable opportunities arose. The disastrous consequence of this policy we have discussed elsewhere. It was left for the statesmen of a later period to evolve a system which while preserving the independence of the Rulers stressed on the duties and responsibilities of paramountcy, and on that basis built up an edifice of co-operative political union in which the British Government as well as the States found their respective places.

The great Indian Rebellion led by dispossessed Princes and their nobility was the end of a period. With it closed the policy of annexation, of treating the Rulers of Indian States as potential enemies waiting for a favourable opportunity to combine against the British Government, enemies whose strength was a source of weakness to the Empire in India and whose activities therefore should be strictly and rigorously watched. The old idea of keeping these States in weakness was abandoned, for it was recognised that the strength and well-being of the States were a guarantee to the peace of India.

The immediate effect of the Mutiny in relation to the States may be stated in one word—the definitive fixation of a policy of treating the States, big, small, important and unimportant, as a part of the Indian polity; and their security, well-being and permanance was acknowledged to be a primary obligation of the British Government.

It is often assumed that with the disappearance of the last vestiges of the Moghul Empire and the assumption of direct authority by the Crown, the Indian Princes became feudatories of the Crown of England as a result of some mystic process by which the pretensions and claims of the descendant of Akbar and Aurangzeb got vested in the new masters of Delhi. This is both historically untrue and logically absurd. The Act of 1858 transferred to the Crown only the rights which the Company possessed. Further it was specifically laid down as the last clause in the Government of India Act that "all treaties made by the Company shall be binding on Her Majesty." The claim of inheritance of Moghul authority is a phantasmagoric fancy of imaginative officers and it has nothing to support it in law or in history.

At the same time the acceptance of the policy of treating Indian States as parts of a single charge, as Lord Canning put it, effected a silent and very significant revolution. The British Government deliberately laid down that in future they do not intend to annex States either on account of misconduct or of disloyalty. Further, they guaranteed the perpetuation of the ruling families by surrendering the discretion they had so far claimed in the matter of permitting adoptions. As a consequence, the Government claimed moral responsibility for the better administration of the States and the right of interference in the affairs of the State in order to secure that end.

The growth of the post-Mutiny policy with regard to Indian States, involving as it does the extension of imperial authority in matters like Railways, Posts and Telegraphs, and the claim of a paramountcy in political and other affairs such as was never put forward before 1857, is beyond our subject. That was but the elaboration of the principle enunciated in 1858 by the Government of India, of treating the States as integral parts of the Empire—parts of a single charge.